The Retailer's Handbook Post COVID-19

Hymie Zawatzky

NOTE:

This is a guide. It is not a substitute for obtaining legal advice about your lease, finances or taxation. Nor is it a replacement for a qualified financial advisor. You are encouraged to seek such legal and financial advice where necessary.

DISCLAIMER

At the time of going to press, all information in this book was accurate as the author was able to ascertain within reason. All references to private or state organisations are gratuitous. The author has no financial interest in them and does nor stand to benefit from them in any way

Veritax Business Consultants Pty Ltd
16 Eildon Street
Doncaster Vic 3108
Australia
WEBSITE: www.placeofbooks.com

Cover Design and typeset by BookPOD
Cover Image: iStockphoto

ISBN: 978-0-9945532-9-4 (pbk)   eISBN: 978-1-922270-54-2 (ebook)

A catalogue record for this book is available from the National Library of Australia

To my wife, Joan

Other titles from the author:

Retail Survival in Tough Times

Retailer's Guide to Carbon Tax

The Immigrant's Guide to Living in Australia

The Immigrant's Guide to Retail

The Retailer's Guide to Lease Negotiation and Administration in Australia

Contents

PART 2: LEASE NEGOTIATION

PART 3: EXITING FROM YOUR BUSINESS

INTRODUCTION

At the time of writing, the impact of Covid-19 is still being felt by retail business and the impact of the virus may continue for years to come.

In this practical guide to retailers, I draw on my many years of experience in retail administration, franchising, leasing and the management of occupancy costs, to help retailers to gain a stronger position in their business, as well as in their negotiations with banks and landlords.

Whether you are an existing retailer, own a retail chain, a new operator from overseas bringing your business to Australia, a professional working in a retail environment or a firsttime migrant retailer seeking a franchise in Australia, this book will I am sure, be of value to you.

Covid-19 has had a major impact on leases and lease negotiation. In an industry dominated by major shopping centre owners it is essential for any retailer to negotiate professionally. A retailer needs to be fully aware of the protection provided under the Retail Tenancy Acts in Australia, as well as to those clauses permitted in leases and those that are not. The relief rental scheme has ended, and all leases will once again be subject to the Tenancy Acts in each state.

The Retailer's Handbook Post Covid-19 will help you in many aspects of negotiation with your landlord including dealing with a situation where a landlord is contemplating relocating your store during the lease term or interfering with the traffic flow to your store during a refurbishment of the shopping centre.

You will gain from the acquiring knowledge on how to administer your lease professionally, from the commencement date to the expiry date. In addition, you will learn how to assess whether the outgoings charged to you by a landlord annually are fair and reasonable. If you wish to exit your business, this book will provide you with the best techniques to do this.

This book will be a useful guide for universities and technical colleges teaching retail studies. Understanding that occupancy costs are among the largest costs of running a retail business. Learning how to control these costs will be invaluable to retail students.

The Retailer's Handbook Post Covid-19 has been written in three parts to make for easy reading, namely:

Financial management

Lease negotiation

Exiting your business

Readers, please note that this book is a guide and not a substitute for obtaining legal advice about your lease should the circumstances require it. You are always encouraged to seek legal and taxation advice where necessary.

SOME IMPORTANT QUESTIONS FOR EVERY RETAILER

If you are presently the owner of a retail business ask yourself:

Are you suffering the effects of Covid-19?

Is the possibility of your renewing your lease for a further five years giving you a headache?

Are you paying too much rent?

Do you wish that you knew how to negotiate a better lease with your landlord?

Do you know how to ensure that the annual outgoings charged by the landlord is fair and reasonable and complies with the provisions of the Retail Tenancy Act in your state?

Are you studying about retail at a college or university?

Do you know the law covering franchisees and franchisors from both a state and federal perspective?

Are you thinking of bringing your business to Australia?

If the answer to any of these questions is "Yes" then this book is for you.

PART 1

FINANCIAL MANAGEMENT

CHAPTER 1

RETAIL RESCUE IN TURBULENT TIMES

It is tough out there for all retailers. Store closures and downsizing of departments by major stores have now become the way of retail in Australia. High rents and the rise of online and mobile phone technology is reshaping retail. The reluctance of consumers to buy products other than at the "best or cheapest price" is having a major impact on small and medium retail businesses as well as on many retail chains that have been in business for many years and have survived downturns in the past.

The covid-19 crises has put additional strains on the profitability of most businesses. Lockdowns have resulted in falls in traffic flow to stores and their profitability. The switch to ecommerce has changed the whole model of most businesses.

Some retailers who have been unable to adapt to the" new way of retail" have unfortunately gone into administration or liquidation.

The financial resources of many retail businesses are limited. Any sustained downturn could well result in the failure of your retail business, irrespective of whether you are a franchisee or run your own business.

But tough circumstances make people tougher. For this reason, making sound financial decisions has never been more important for you as a retailer, and for the survival of your business. Are you going to leave it to accountants and bankers to measure your performance in the past week or month, or are you going to take control?

You can adapt to changes, take control and keep your business healthy and growing, by introducing simple but important steps of key performance measurement indicators. These indicators will take minimal time to implement but they will let you know that your business is still healthy. They will allow you to plan and market for the future and help you to decide on any necessary steps to correct past mistakes earlier rather than later.

There is no quick fix to your problems. The financial survival and health of your retail business will only be achieved through continuous management and control applied according to a plan backed up by sound knowledge of basic financial issues and changing retail circumstances. As always, knowledge is power.

Of course, there are still crucial financial matters to discuss with your accountant or solicitor on an annual basis, but the persistent and constant control of the management of your business is up to you. It is you only and your team of trusted advisors who can keep your business afloat in these uncertain times.

To survive in retail and flourish in the current climate, you need to address the following vital questions and ask yourself if they apply to your business:

- What can I do about my situation? Is there an immediate health check that I can apply to my business?
- Is there any action I can take in my store to counter the expanding operations of competing websites and the growth of ecommerce?
- Does my business look as if it may like close or go into receivership? If so, what are the implications for me and my family?
- If I have too much stock at the start of the year, how do I lower the stock level to acceptable levels by Christmas?
- Given the downturn in the economy, is my rent is too high? If so, how can I negotiate with my landlord for some assistance?
- While negotiating the renewal of my lease during an economic downturn are there negotiating techniques and concessions I can implement that will stand me in good stead when the recession ends?
- If my lease calls for the refurbishment of my business this year, how can I convince the bank to give me a loan?

- How can I prepare and monitor my cash flow statements to take early action ahead of any cash crises?
- Do the ratios in my balance sheet and profit and loss statements give my bank manager, suppliers, landlords or my franchisor, confidence to continue supporting me through this difficult time?
- Am I getting the most from my advertising dollar?
- How can I plan to mark down goods to generate extra sales?
- Am I maximizing my profit from each square metre of space in my store?
- If my business looks as if it will make a loss, can I reduce costs to keep afloat without wrecking my business completely?

Are you satisfied by your answers to these questions?

If you are not, is there something you can do to improve your situation?

In the following chapters of this book, you will find answers and information that will assist you and ensure the continuous health of your business.

CHAPTER 3

ONLINE SHOPPING AND MOBILE PHONE TECHNOLOGY IN YOUR RETAIL STORE

One of today's biggest challenges for retailers as an outcome of Covid-19 is the rise of internet and mobile phone online buying.

Consumers have now realised that for many years they may have paid too much for their goods. The rise of online buying has shown them that by surfing the net they can buy the same branded products overseas for very much less than in Australian stores, even with the added cost of postage. Unfortunately, the fall in value of the Australian dollar against the American dollar has been substantial and this trend has diminished substantially.

The consumer does not even have to leave the comfort of his homes to buy online. He or she has an amazingly wide range of products to choose from, far more than you could ever stock in your store. And with a click of a button, they can buy with "Paylater" and even manage payments more easily.

Let's look at this new trend and decide how we can turn the situation to our advantage.

THE IMPACT OF INTERNET BUYING ON SHOPPING CENTRES AND RETAILERS

In the case of large shopping centres, many small retailers and chains who rely on the traffic flow generated by the anchor tenants like department stores are feeling the pinch Many have closed because of the Covid-19 epidemic. The department stores themselves are starting to feel pressured by the growth of internet and mobile phone shopping.

Without a strong department store to draw traffic flow, landlords of these centres, are now focussing on reinventing speciality stores from whom they receive most of their rental income. Some commentators have even suggested that this shift in demand may eventually result in shopping centres looking more like theme parks than traditional shopping centres.

The latest figures clearly show that consumers are spending less in department stores. While many in the past 20 years have predicted the end of the department store retailer, somehow, they are still trading.

However, they have decided to change the mix of merchandise in their stores. Gone are whitegoods and other big-ticket items that once sold well, and they are replaced by increased offerings of fashion, cosmetics, and gifts. Small retailers in shopping centres are now forced to contend with the changes made by the department stores and adapt accordingly.

Since the recent downturn, consumers have become more cautious and concerned about saving as much as possible for that rainy day. This change in attitude means that "easy go shopping" and putting a string of retail purchases on credit is a thing of the past. Today's consumer is more likely to spend cautiously, check prices carefully on the internet, buy on eftpos instead of on their credit card, and even put money away in the bank . Higher bills for electricity and bus fares, have also contributed to this state of mind of the consumer.

HOW CAN RETAILERS TURN THIS NEW FORM OF CONSUMMER SPENDING TO THEIR ADVANTAGE?

More and more people are using ecommerce, the internet, and social media. The language of buying has changed and people respond as they do on Facebook. They have become used to pressing "like" "share" or "comment" buttons to make their opinions known. As it is the customer who calls the tune, you the retailer will have to keep up with these new trends. Let us now look at how to take advantage of these new trends in customer spending:

- Create a store website of your store with online capabilities and with your products and prices clearly and attractively displayed. This will turn your store into a giant catalogue.
- Ideally, every retail business should have the following online essential software:
  - A website that you can update yourself.
  - An email marketing newsletter that you can post to subscribers through the internet.
  - A blog that you can connect to your website and to your Facebook fan page.
- A good idea is to offer loyalty programs, discounts or coupons on your site to prevent your customers checking prices with their mobile phones and buying from your competitor.
- You should make certain that you focus on finely targeted individual sales instead of mass sales.
- It is essential that you ensure that your supply chain logistics and inventory management are perfect. You dare not run out of stock or customers will search elsewhere to buy.

Remember that unlike overseas internet sites, you will still so have to bear the costs of delivery and GST, so price your products accordingly.

- Be certain that your security measures on mobile phone transactions are of the highest quality, as customers continue to be concerned about the security of their transactions.
- Do your utmost to create something innovative with the presentation of your product. Some stores allow the iPhone to select a piece of furniture from the catalogue and using the phone's camera, place it anywhere in the room and then change its size to fit the perspective.
- A large fashion store in the UK allows the customer to select a dress, hold it up to her body and then look in a mirror. The garment is then imposed on the image in the mirror to show how the dress fits on the customer. All this without having to go into the store's change room.
- It is essential that staff training is orientated to customer needs. If a

customer requests help, staff must know their products, be courteous and friendly to the person online and makes the customer feel welcome, Retailers may have to ensure that staff authorised to take calls have the proper training. In addition, the techniques of add-on selling and closing the sale before the customer goes elsewhere, are vital.

- The use of a "chat line" where customers can ask for help with difficulties in using your website or if they are uncertain about materials used in products, or a size is suggested.
- A small gift of chocolate or similar, accompanying a delivery will be appreciated by customers buying on your website for the first time. And they may be more likely to buy from you again.
- Make sure that your website is constantly up to date. Do not advertise products that will only be delivered to customers in 3 weeks. Delays annoy customers and they may not come back to your site.
- You should encourage every customer to contribute to and be part of your monthly email newsletter. Expressing their opinions about your site or your products makes them feel part of your organisation and important.
- It is a good idea to form alliances with other complimentary retailers and showcase each other. Create your own collective VIP cards and promote each other in your newsletters. These days retailers need to stick together, and networking is an excellent means of survival.

If you adopt these measures, you will give your customers not only a rewarding channel to buy products, but encourage their loyalty to your store. Even more importantly, it will give retailers the opportunity to talk to their customers in real time.

There will always be those customers who want to see and feel what they are buying. Many people still want and need the help and advice of a salesperson when buying. Online buying on the internet and the use of mobile smartphones will not end conventional retail as there is still place for bricks and mortar, but online buying is undoubtably shaping the customers experience and will reshape the consumer experience.

The retailer's staff should acquire a knowledge of crypto currency and its use in future retail business.

CHAPTER 4

IN THE CURRENT UPHEAVAL IN RETAIL, IS YOUR BUSINESS STILL HEALTHY? DO YOU NEED A DOCTOR?

Below is a checklist of questions with explanations which clearly outline the risk that your business faces if these answers are not adequately addressed.

Read the list carefully and you will find that it provides you with an idea of the areas in which your business needs the most attention. It will prove to be an extremely important document as it pinpoints key problem areas. Remember to take this list with you when you visit your accountant.

THE BUSINESS HEALTH CHECKLIST TO BE ANSWERED BY EVERY SMALL BUSINESS OWNER SO THE RISKS CAN BE ASSESSED

Question 1:

Is your lease healthy?

If not, carefully read part 2 of this handbook. A poor lease could have a major impact on your future business.

Question 2:

Have you given any personal guarantees during the year? If so, were they blanket guarantees, or did you put only certain personal assets at risk?

In the event of a default all your personal assets could be taken.

Question 3:

Does your business structure protect your personal or family assets? Are you a company, a family trust, or a private personal operator?

Different structures have different levels of personal liability and must be viewed individually.

Question 4:

Are you maintaining adequate liability insurance in the event of a claim?

If you are held to be negligent, you, as the business owner can be held liable regardless of your company structure.

Question 5:

Are you depositing all your income? Are your records in sufficient order to sustain a GST audit?

The tax office can and will fine you and could even try to take possession of your personal assets.

Question 6:

If you are in a partnership, do you have a current buy-sell agreement in place, in the event of the death or disability of one of the partners?

Forced liquidation of the business could result from the absence of such an agreement.

Question 7:

If you have a family business, have all parties agreed in writing to their responsibilities and do they understand what this means?

Disharmony in a family and business can result in poor business practice and inadequate management decisions.

Question 8:

Have you given adequate attention to the issues of retirement and superannuation planning and possibly the issue of business succession?

Everyone is subject to old age and possible ill health. Creditors will be more at ease if the business has a succession plan in place and long-term debt repayment is assured.

Question 9:

Are all directors' loans adequately documented representing an arms length transaction?

Debit balances on directors' loans may be classified by the tax office as dividends.

Question 10:

In the event of your lease expiring, have you ensured that you will have sufficient funds to both meet the cost of refitting your shop and the cost of paying for possible large rental increases?

Major rental increases or substantial capital costs for refitting of premises can put pressure on cash flow and business profitability.

Question 11:

Have you conducted a full stock check recently? Does your business appear to have much stock shrinkage?

Stock shrinkage reduces gross profit and can have a major impact on cash flow.

Question 12:

Is the technology in your business, such as point of sale equipment, internet access to your products and website, in line with the latest available equipment?

Inability to obtain instant information and analysis of sales or the inability of customers to contact you from outside your premises could soon result in loss of sales.

SOME QUICK ACTION TIPS IF YOU SAID "NO" TO ANY OF THE PREVIOUS TWELVE QUESTIONS:

Guarantees:

If you are asked to give a personal guarantee on a lease for your premises, as is usual in any leasing transaction, always try to put a cap on your exposure.

For example, insert a clause in the guarantee document, limiting the personal guarantee to possibly three months rental. This should then be sufficient time for a landlord to re-let the premises.

If you run your business as a company, the Australian Corporations Law allows companies to function with one director. Even if you or your wife and children are the owners or shareholders in the business, only appoint one of the family as the director. This will shield other members of the family from having to give personal or director's guarantees.

Business Structure

If you have more than one small business, and for example you own two businesses, it is important to have each business as a separate legal entity. This will prevent creditors in one business trying to attach the assets in the other business for the payment of any outstanding debts.

If you have a registered trade, brand, or product name, by which your business is known, and that has cost you considerable amounts of advertising dollars to be instantly recognised by the public, it is good sense to have that trade name registered in a shelf company or trust.

This entity should be separate from your normal business, with no assets or liabilities other than that name. Then if you go broke in that company, you will still own the trade name, and in time you will be able to start up again.

CHAPTER 5

KEY PERFORMANCE INDICATORS FOR RETAILERS TO TEST THE VIABILITY OF THEIR BUSINESS

To keep your business healthy, especially in tough times, you need to keep a sharp eye on its performance.

The two best performance measurement criteria that should be used by speciality small business retail operators in tough times are:

A. The measurement of the business stock turn
B. Break Even Analysis

A. STOCK TURN OVER

What do we mean by stock turnover?

Stock turnover is defined as the number of times during a specific period, usually one year, that the stock on hand is sold.

At times such as the present, slow stock turn means that your cash flow is not being turned into money to pay your creditors. The stock is simply lying on the shelves. If this continues for too long, it is a recipe for quick bankruptcy.

In addition to building up your cash flow, a high level of stock turnover in a business has several advantages for any retailer: Remember your store has a limited amount of space.

It must always be your objective to get the most profit per square foot out of your valuable space. Slow movers tie up valuable space.

Some advantages of high stock turns are as follows:

- Merchandise on the shelves is always fresh and keeps customers interested.
- Losses due to changes in technology are reduced.
- Costs associated with maintaining stock, such as interest, insurance, and breakage are all reduced.
- You can take advantage of discounts offered by suppliers.

THE FORMULA FOR CALCULATING YOUR STOCK TURN

Most retailers who keep computerized records of their merchandise at cost price use this reliable cost price method of calculation.

Take the cost of goods sold during the year and divide them by the average cost of your stock on hand,

To calculate your stock turn:

$$\text{Stock Turn} = \frac{\text{Cost of goods sold during the year}}{\text{Average stock on hand (at cost)}}$$

You will find this information is readily available from your trading account so the calculation is easy to do.

More often end of year stock figures are used for this calculation (instead of averages) but there are advantages to using averages of the stock holding at both the start and the end of the year. Levelling out high and low stock levels held during peaks or slow months will give you the yearly average.

TIP:

As different businesses have different levels of stock turn, you should always try to ensure that you are in line with other retailers selling similar products. It would be useless to compare your stock turn with that of a fashion store or hardware store, if you own a camera store.

SO HOW CAN YOU AS A SMALL RETAILER MAXIMISE THE STOCK TURN IN YOUR BUSINESS?

If you are not achieving the average turnover that is applicable for your industry, or would like to improve your stock turnover, these are some useful ideas that you could adopt:

- Identify your best-selling items promptly.
- Eliminate, if possible, slow selling items.
- Reduce your range so that you ensure your optimum range contains your strongest and most profitable product groups.
- Maintain a minimal stock of" have to keep lines".
- Buy in an efficient and timely manner.
- Only do business with reliable distributors.
- Allocate prime selling positions in your store to your best-selling classifications.

BREAK EVEN SALES

What does the term break even sales mean?

Break even sales is defined by accountants as "that level of sales at which the gross profit on sales will recover the total expenses of the store." Over this level, the net profit of the store will be equal to the gross profit on excess sales. This means that at the break-even level of sales, you have made sufficient gross profit from trading to cover all the expenses of your store, such as rent and salaries for that month or period.

One of the most important calculations that every retailer should make each month, is to determine the break-even sales of that store. In the current difficult climate with funds tight, this is even more essential than usual. Once you have established your break-even figure, it is extremely easy to make an estimate of your profit or loss for the month without having to wait for your accountant to do the calculation.

This is how you calculate your break-even sales:

Your costs for the month are divided into variable expenses and fixed expenses.

Variable expenses are those which vary directly with turnover, for instance salaries and wages. Most monthly expenses that you will have are *fixed expenses,* apart from any casual staff wages.

For this break-even analysis technique, the total expenses for the month can be considered as fixed costs.

FORMULA FOR BREAK EVEN SALES

$$\text{BREAK EVEN SALES} = \frac{\text{TOTAL FIXED COSTS}}{\text{GROSS PROFIT}}$$

Example:

Let us assume that you, a retailer, have a gross profit margin of, say, 34% on sales over a number of years and that your budgeted expenses for the month of June was $21150

Calculate your break even sales as follows:

$$\text{Break even sales for month} = \frac{\text{Total expenses}}{\%\text{ Gross Margin}} \times \frac{100.}{1}$$

$$= \frac{21{,}150}{0.34} \times \frac{100}{1}$$

$$= \$\,62{,}205 \text{ for month}$$

This means that at a level of sales of $62,205 you will make a gross profit of

$62,205 x 34%	$21,150
Less Total Expenses for month	$21,150
Net Profit	Nil

According to the above example, all sales greater than $62,205 for the month multiplied by your gross margin will give you your net profit for the month.

If you went to your accountant with the same level of expenses of $21150, and the gross profit that you usually achieve of 34%, together with a sales figure for the month of $100000, (which was made for the months achieved), your accountant will present you with a profit and loss account which looks like this:

Sales	$100,000
Gross Profit (34% of $100,000) =	$34,000
Less Expenses	$21,150
Net Profit for Month	$12,850

You do not need to wait for your accountant; you can make your own simple calculation in the following manner:

Sales for Month	$100,000
Less Break-Even Sales	$62,205
Difference	$37,795

Net profit for month
= $ 37,795 X 34 %   = $ 12850

When your accountant meets with you, he will simply verify your calculation.

This formula is also useful when you need to calculate the extra sales in your business to pay for an additional expense. Have a look at the following helpful examples

Example 1

Your store manager suggests an advertising campaign on your website to boost sales. The campaign could cost about $10000.

If you divide $10000 by 34% (the same gross percentage as previously) you will discover that you need the following amount of extra sales to pay for it:

See the calculation below:

$$\frac{10000}{0.34}$$

$$= \quad \$29412 \text{ extra sales}$$

This calculation allows you to make essential choices.

If the proposed expense does not look like achieving more than $29412 worth of extra sales, then it seems reasonable not to go ahead with the advertising campaign.

If you reduce each extra cost *to the number of sales* that you need to recover it, as per the formula above, everyone working in your store will understand the formula.

In addition, if you evaluate every additional expense in this way, you will be able to determine the extra sales you will require to pay for any new expense that comes up. Though this seems like a very rigid test and may not always be practical, at a time of cost containment, when sales are falling, it is likely to be your best approach.

Example 2

If the sales in your store are falling and you must let go a staff member who earns approximately $25000 per annum, the following calculation will be useful.

You divide $25000 by your gross profit of 34% = $73530

This will allow your sales to fall by $73530 per annum as a set off for reducing the staff member earning $25000 per annum.

Example 3

You are paying a rental of $100000 per annum and you have a 5% automatic rental increase of $5000 on the anniversary date of the lease. On the day, your rental goes up, you can calculate the amount your future sales will need to increase, to offset the rental increase as follows:

$5000 divided by your gross profit percentage of 34% or $14705 per annum to cover this rental increase.

However, in a tough retail climate where sales may be falling due to increased competition, Covid-19, or due to rising on-line purchases, it may not be possible to increase your sales. You may even have to ask the landlord to forgo the increase.

CHAPTER 6

BENCHMARKING YOUR BUSINESS

A key method of ensuring that your overall trading performance is and remains competitive, is by benchmarking your business (also known as KPI's) against retail industry sector comparisons and standards.

Utilisation of the information gained from this will allow you to identify the productivity and efficiency of your retail business and provide you with guidelines for achieving improvement.

Variations between any individual results, best practice, and the overall industry sector standards, can be adjusted by putting into place a corrective action plan.

A FINANCIAL BENCHMARKING ANALYSIS AND REPORT

This type of report would generally cover the following questions:

Profitability

What gross and net margins should your business be able to achieve?

Return on investment

Is your business providing an adequate return on the money invested?

Business risk

What is the gross break-even figure that your business is required to achieve on a weekly/monthly or yearly basis?

What drop in revenue could your business absorb before incurring losses?

Efficiency

Are the level of your expenses too high relative to businesses of a similar size?

How efficient are the costs of your business?

Productivity

Are your staff generating enough revenue for each dollar of labour spent?

Is your business generating adequate income per square metre of floor space?

Stock control

What level of stock are businesses like yours holding to achieve a similar level of sales?

What stock turn level is required to ensure maximum stock control?

Is your business generating an adequate gross margin return on inventory?

Example:

In this example let us look at the benchmarking analysis for footwear retailers last produced by an EBC Business Benchmarking for larger stores in shopping centres, together with some recent performance benchmarks produced by the Australian Taxation office.

Understanding the analysis used in this particular business will help you to apply the principles used, to your own business. You will also gain a better understanding of benchmarking as a technique.

The following points emerge from the analysis:

- Personnel productivity and stock management are the two critical areas in footwear retail.
- High personnel productivity keeps a major cost, namely wages, under control.
- Stock management is critical. Having this year's fashion in stock is vital. Not being left at the end of the season with sizes that are large or too small is essential.

The most profitable shoe businesses in their survey showed the following:

- Stores were larger. But this may not still be valid as ecommerce requirements are totally different as regards space for administration and storage of stock.
- They had a much higher personnel productivity. This showed that staff were motivated to sell, working effectively converting sales into enquiries and "up selling".
- Stores had a better stock productivity.
- Stores had higher stock turn coupled with higher gross profit margins.
- Stores generated more revenue from each dollar of assets.
- Owners of stores worked more hours per year.

Benchmarks for the footwear industry from these two sources were as follows:

	Average
Gross Profit	49.88%
Interest Bank Charges etc as a percentage of sales	3.99%
% rent to sales (non-shopping centre)	9.72%
% wages and salaries (staff only not owners) to sales	15.7%
% net profit before owner's salary and benefits to sales	20.51%
Stock turn Rate per annum	3.05 times
Sales and Display area as a percentage of Total Area	75%
Total sales generated per person working In the store	$204245
Advertising Promotion (including franchise fees)	2.90%
Insurance	2.42%
Other occupancy Costs	2.45%
Depreciation, lease costs and Hire purchase	4.20%

When it comes to shopping centres the cost of rent and outgoings rises very substantially

CHAPTER 7

MARGINS, MARKUPS AND MARKDOWNS

Confusion can lead to bankruptcy without you, the business owner, knowing it.

The failure to fully understand and utilize the important business concepts *of margins, mark ups and mark downs* and the part they play in managing a retail business, can damage your business and even result in its collapse without you realising it,

Ask yourself if you are you in control of these three vital concepts or if they are slipping from your grasp. Let us examine them carefully:

1. WHAT ARE MARK UPS?

A Mark Up is the *difference* between the *cost price* and *selling price* of an item. It is expressed as a *percentage of cost price*:

It is calculated as follows:

$$\text{Mark up} = \frac{\text{Selling price - Cost Price}}{\text{Cost price}} \times 100$$

Example: If we buy a handbag for $60 and decide to sell it for $ 90

Then according to the formula: -

$$\text{Mark up} \quad = \quad \frac{\$90 - \$60}{\$60} \quad x \quad 100$$

$$= \quad \frac{30 \times 100}{60}$$

$$= \quad 50.0\%$$

2. WHAT DO WE MEAN BY MARGINS?

The margin is the *difference* between the *cost price* and the *selling price* and is expressed as a *percentage of the selling price*.

It is calculated as follows:

$$\text{Margin} \quad = \quad \frac{\text{Selling price - Cost Price}}{\text{Selling price}} \quad x \quad 100$$

Therefore, in our example of the handbag:

$$\text{Margin} \quad = \quad \frac{\$90 - \$60}{\$90} \quad x \quad 100$$

$$= \quad \frac{30 \times 100}{90}$$

$$= \quad 33.33\%$$

It is important to note that though there is a complimentary relationship between mark ups and margins, the margin is always the smaller of the two figures.

When we talk about the gross profit you are making, we are talking about the margin you are making on the sale. These two terms, *gross profit and margin, are one and the same.*

TIP

Given that you know the desired mark up, there is a quick table that can be used to compare the margin with the gross profit made on a product.

% Mark up on cost of product	% Gross Profit or margin on Sales Price
10.0	9.0
11.1	10.0
20.0	16.7
25.0	20.0
33.3	25.0
50.0	33.3
66.7	40.0
75.0	42.8
90.0	47.3
100.0	50.0

The mark up you decide to use depends on your approach to pricing and your type of business. Some businesses tend to have high mark-ups and low turnover, whilst others tend to have low mark-ups and a high turnover.

3. WHAT DO WE MEAN BY MARKDOWNS?

A Mark Down is defined as the *difference* between the *original selling* price and the *new selling* price. It is expressed as a *percentage* of that original selling price.

Example:

If an item sells for $90 and after three months you decide to mark down its selling price to $70:

$$Mark\ down = \frac{\$90 - \$70}{\$90} \times 100$$

$$= \frac{20 \times 100}{90}$$

$$= 22.2\%$$

There are occasions during a year, particularly in the current economic climate, when money is tight, and people have become very price conscious. Buyers may be comparing your price for a product. If your product is discounted to meet the online price, then they will tend to buy from you.

In this situation you may be marking down your stock either to clear slow-moving merchandise or to stimulate sales. Markdowns are likely to stimulate extra sales if the increase in sales is insufficient, not only will your overall profitability be affected, but the expected gross profit of your business will fall.

It is important to bear in mind that sales and price reductions go hand in glove. Be sure that you know the exact impact of price cutting on your profitability.

The following table is a guide to help you calculate the increased sales you will need to make in order to compensate for various price reductions.

Percentage increases in sales necessary to break even after a price cut

Price Cut	Present Gross Profit Margin (%)							
	10	20	30	40	50	60	70	80
5%	100	33.3	20.0	14.3	11.1	9.1	7.7	6.7
10%		100.0	50.0	33.3	25.0	20.0	16.7	14.3
15%		300.0	100.0	60.0	42.9	33.3	27.3	23.1
20%			200.0	100.0	66.7	50.0	40.0	33.3
25%			500.0	166.7	100.0	71.4	55.6	45.5
30%				300.0	150.0	100.0	75.0	60.0
35%				700.0	233.3	140.0	100.0	77.8
40%					400.0	200.0	133.3	100.0
50%						400.0	250.0	166.7

Example:

If you usually sell a pair of boots for $100 that cost you $60, and you make a profit of $40, the gross profit percentage to sales is 40 %.

Assume you sell 50 pairs of boots per year, and you will make a gross profit on those boots for the year of:

50 x $ 40 = $2000

If you decide to mark down the shoes by 20 % for a sale and you propose to sell the boots for $80. By following the table you will find that if the gross margin is 40% and you want to cut the price by 20%, the increase in sales necessary to break even after the price cut is 100.0%.

Therefore, to maintain your total gross profit dollars on that line of boots you will have to increase your sales by 100%.

See the following example:

Normal quantity sold 50	Sale quantity required 100
Normal Profit per pair $40	Sale profit per Pair $20
Normal gross profit Dollars earned $2000	Sale Gross Profit Dollars earned $2000

4. BUDGETING FOR AND MONITORING MARKDOWNS

In the current economic climate in retailing, markdowns are a fact of life. Whether we like it or not, despite the buying of merchandise becoming more sophisticated, it is still subject to buyer error.

So, how do we measure the performance of our buyers?

Changing fashions and colours, or ordering too much of a particular product can result in markdowns being required to sell your merchandise.

If you accept this as a fact, you can set up a budget to monitor markdowns to determine just how effective your buying has been.

Obviously, if your markdowns are greater than you originally thought, this will have a major impact on your profits. If they are lower than you thought, you will see the effect on the bottom-line profit.

Setting the budget will be of no value unless, at the same time, you set up a method of estimating the value of proposed markdowns from your normal prices. This is simpler to do than it looks.

You will find that there are many available computer programs to do this for you. But if you prefer to operate a calculator manually, and use an analysis book, it can do the job just as well.

5. *PREPARING A MARK-DOWN BUDGET*

To set up your budget for markdowns for next season you need the following accounting information.

1. The projected monthly sales for your store, or if applicable by department.
2. Your mark-up on products that will allow you to calculate your "1st margin on sales." This refers to the gross profit on sales if all goods were sold at full margin.
3. The final gross profit you expect to show in your accounts after markdown.

The following example clearly demonstrates an accounting budget and a markdown budget.

	$	%
ACCOUNTING BUDGET		
Sales Budget - Net	1000	100
Cost of Sales	600	60
Gross Profit	400	40
MARKDOWN BUDGET		
Mark up on all Goods	100%	
Gross Profit at Full Margin	50%	

TIP

It is important to remember that the cost of sales will remain unchanged irrespective of whether you are having markdowns or not.

For example, if all goods were sold at the full mark-up of 100 % on cost, you would have achieved theoretical sales for the year of:

$$600 + 100\% \text{ of } \$600 = \$1200$$

Therefore, you can make the following calculation:

% Mark-downs for the year	=	$\dfrac{\text{Theoretical Sales - Actual sales}}{\text{Theoretical Sales}}$ x 100

$$= \frac{(\$1200 - \$1000)}{1200} \times 100$$

$$= \frac{200}{1200} \times 100$$

$$= 16.67\%$$

The above example shows that you are budgeting for markdowns with a sales value of $200 for the year. Having a mark down budget figure provides you with access to further valuable information.

If you multiply the selling price of a product with the number of products sold during the year, you will be able to calculate the actual value of your markdowns. This is an extremely valuable figure for your budgeting.

If you compare the actual value with your budgeted value of markdowns, you will then be able to measure the efficiency of the buying department and their ability to obtain the margins on products that the company expects to achieve.

CHAPTER 8

USING THE SAME FINANCIAL RATIOS AS YOUR BANK USES TO TAKE THE TEMPERATURE OF YOUR BUSINESS

You will find that in difficult times, the only way your bank manager will continue to give you an overdraft and other borrowing facilities, is if you comply with his set of ratios and analysis of your accounts. In this way you will be able to convince him that you will be able to repay the money lent to you.

Your balance sheet and profit income statement represent a complete financial record of your business. Together with the other financial information you gather on a weekly or monthly basis, you can develop a set of measurements that will independently allow you to monitor both your current position and your progress. Armed with this information, you will be in the driver's seat when you come to face a similar analysis by your bank.

You can develop this invaluable set of business measurements through a series of financial relationships or ratios.

WHAT DO WE MEAN BY RATIOS?

A *ratio* is nothing more than one number in relation to another. For example, the relationship of 2 to 1. Or the relationship can be expressed as a percentage, such as gross profit of 35% of turnover.

WHAT IS THE VALUE OF RATIOS FOR A RETAILER?

The importance of the ratio is its ability to measure and manage your financial effectiveness. Without it you will be operating by guesswork.

READING THE RATIO THERMOMETER

Financial ratios in isolation have little significance. They only have significance when comparisons are made with past or future ratios, or comparisons with competitors, industry standards or a comparison with "rule of thumb" standards. This comparison provides the window for you to see into your business and develop ways to improve its operation.

Especially in tough times like these, financial ratios can tell you about the stress and strains that are at work in your business. They mesh like the gears in your motorcar, to propel your business forward. Not knowing your ratios is a little like the first time you attempt to drive a manual car – a bumpy ride at best.

One necessary set of ratios that we use is known as Key Performance Ratios. They assist us in analyzing the liquidity, the profitability and efficiency of the business. In tough business times, these ratios are particularly important, especially to bankers, in assessing your overdraft facilities or in the granting of an additional bank loan.

CARING FOR YOUR BUSINESS

In line with the theme of treating your business like you would care for the health of your own body, ratio analysis is equivalent to taking the temperature of the business.

Ratio Analysis is an excellent method for determining the overall financial condition of a small business and its ability of surviving the current retail crises. It puts information from your financial statement into perspective and it helps you to spot financial patterns that may threaten the health of your business.

Even though management accounting is often clouded in mystique, you can analyse and interpret financial statements yourself. And one of the most widely practiced ways is using financial ratios.

Make a diagnosis to assess which ratio will perform best for you.

The question that each small businessperson needs to establish is **"which relationship to measure. "**

THE DIFFERENT RATIOS AND HOW TO CALCULATE THEM

First decide on the questions you want to ask about the performance of your business. Then look at the various means of calculating them by using one of the simple ratios. Once you decide on the type of ratio your business needs the rest is straightforward.

To do this you need sufficient information to get the job done without it becoming confusing.

> **Remember that no individual ratio tells the entire story. Taken together however, ratios allow you to begin the process of analysing your business performance and even more important, planning.**

In general, ratios can be used to analyse your business by:

- Comparing the current performance to prior years – giving you the business trends. Consider the drop in business in 2020 as a result of Covid-19.
- Comparing your present performance to other retailers in your field.
- Comparing your ratios with your budget or plans so that you can develop a working strategy for the future.

THE LINK BETWEEN THE TWO FINANCIAL STATEMENTS

One component that measures the functioning of the business and its health through the inter-relationship of the balance sheet and income statement is *efficiency.*

Efficiency is the technique of converting assets (like stock) to revenue, converting revenue to profits and structuring liabilities and net worth so that you can use borrowed money as well as your own, to finance your business.

Your bank manager probably applies all the ratios indicated below when he examines your financial records.

TYPES OF RATIOS

The steps you need to take to analyse your business:

Gather all the accurate financial information available in the business for the past two or three years. This may be difficult for some people following Covid-19.

- Set out these statements on a spread sheet format side by side.
- Now you are ready to use that same spread sheet to calculate the ratios.

BALANCE SHEET RATIOS

There are two balance sheet ratios that you need to know about– current ratios and quick ratios.

CURRENT RATIO

This ratio measures not only the solvency of your business but also your business' ability to pay short-term debts. This is done by comparing the current assets and current liabilities of your business.

It is particularly important if you are thinking of borrowing money from your bank or obtaining substantial credit from a supplier.

Changes in your current ratio over several years could indicate financial problems on the horizon. The key is to find out why the ratio has changed.

HOW TO CALCULATE A CURRENT RATIO:

Current Assets (Stock + Debtors +Cash)
Current Liabilities (trade creditors + short term borrowings + overdraft)

HOW DOES THIS PARTICULAR RATIO MEASURE THE HEALTH OF YOUR BUSINESS IN DOLLARS AND CENTS?

This is the "rule of thumb" ratio used by bankers to measure the solvency of your business. The current ratio should be expressed as approximately 2 to 1. (Your total current assets are twice your current liabilities). Note that businesses with growing sales and a short operating cycle in turning over their stock, can work well with a lower ratio than 2 to 1.

However, given the unpredictability of the selling cycle of retailing, particularly in the current climate, you should not allow yourself to be held to these terms by bankers, as you may not be able to pay your suppliers or take advantage of discounts for cash.

What does this ratio mean – in terms of your business' own performance and industry standards?

If it is too high: This may indicate an imbalance in your investment in long term assets or it can show an economic situation developing, which is conducive to maintaining high liquidity.

If you have a high cash balance you should take advantage of a major price decrease. On the other hand, it could show an overstocked warehouse.

If it is too low: This may indicate that you are financing long term assets with short-term money.

QUICK RATIO

This ratio (sometimes known as the "acid test" ratio) measures the liquidity of the business – your ability to raise cash quickly if pressed by suppliers. It is like the current ratio, but the difference is that stock is not taken into account.

Stock does not always sell quickly and including it in such a calculation could distort the figures.

Potential creditors like to use a quick ratio instead of the current ratio because it reveals the business' ability to pay off trade debt under the worst possible conditions, such as at a time of recession.

HOW TO CALCULATE A QUICK RATIO

$$\frac{\text{Cash + accounts receivable}}{\text{Current Liabilities}}$$

What this means in dollars and cents:

This ratio may be used by a supplier, in a situation where the business places an abnormally high order or when the supplier has in the past not been paid on time. Most suppliers know that on a quick sale, stock only achieves 20% -30 % of its value. Hence the need for this ratio.

The rule of thumb for the quick ratio is 1 to 1. However, this rule of thumb needs to be interpreted with care, particularly for retailers who operate on cash or credit cards with stock as their major asset.

How do you interpret this ratio in terms of your business' performance and industry standards?

If it is too high: This may indicate an excess of cash. Normally it implies an under-investment in stock, and it shows up in reduced sales and reduced profits. This occurs because you do not have enough stock to sell and your customers are likely to go elsewhere.

If it is too low: It may manifest itself in a shortage of cash. It usually indicates financing of long-term assets with short-term money or problems associated with an over investment in stock.

INCOME STATEMENT RATIOS

PROFITABILITY RATIOS

Every retailer wants to know if their business is profitable. Therefore, calculating the key ratios pertaining to your profit and loss account, is a critical piece of information available.

The absolute level of profit may provide an indication of the size of your business, but on its own it says extraordinarily little about the performance of your business.

To evaluate your level of profit, your profit must be compared and related to other aspects of your business.

Profitability ratios will inevitability reflect the business environment of the time. Again, comparisons with other businesses in the same industry segment will provide an indication of management's relative ability to perform in the same business and economic environment.

Profitability ratios consist of two types:

1. The first is profitability compared with sales, which show how well each dollar of your sales generates profit.
2. The second is profitability compared with assets. This determines how hard your assets are working to generate profit.

1. THE GROSS MARGIN RATIO

This ratio measures the profitability of the business at the gross profit level.

For example, a gross margin of 35% means that for every $1 of sales the business produces 35 cents gross profit.

Some business owners will use the anticipated gross profit to help them price their products or services. Whilst some factors, like competition and demand, play a part in pricing decisions, a gross profit measurement is a good starting point in product pricing.

HOW TO CALCULATE A GROSS MARGIN RATIO

$$\frac{\text{Gross profit}}{\text{Sales}}$$

What does this ratio mean if compared to your business' own performance and industry standards?

If it is too high: This means the business is earning its full mark-up without resorting to discounting to clear stock. However, a policy of not discounting could result in a very much slower stock turn with out-of-date stock still sitting on shelves.

If it is too low: This should be of concern to you. A low gross margin usually represents a reduction in sale prices. This reduction may occur through markdowns or an increase in cost of sales that may not have been passed on to customers by shrinkage, not taking discounts due to excessive stock or low cash. It may even be caused by matching prices with a competitor or trying to gain market share at a price.

2. THE NET MARGIN RATIO

This ratio represents the average net profit earned by each dollar of your sales.

It represents the operating profit of the business. Or it be the amount left from your sales dollar after deducting your cost of goods sold (that is your gross profit) and your ordinary operating cost of doing business.

Your operating percentage simply tells you the percentage of your sales that will turn into profit. Again, reductions in this percentage might indicate the need to re-evaluate your pricing, your suppliers or you need to look for other ways of cutting down on your operating costs.

HOW TO CALCULATE THE NET MARGIN RATIO

$$\frac{\text{Net Profit before Tax}}{\text{Sales}}$$

What does this ratio mean when you compare it to your business' own performance and industry standards?

If it is too high: This means the business has been able to contain its overheads, like salaries, wages and occupancy costs which are fixed costs, irrespective of the level of sales.

If it is too low: This is of serious concern as it shows that expenses that have risen substantially during the year have not been offset by the necessary increases in sales. To survive you will have to address expenses very carefully, particularly labour and occupancy costs.

3. THE OCCUPANCY COST RATIO:

This ratio measures the occupancy cost of your business. It determines the amount of rent your business can afford to pay.

A rule of thumb is that the percentage should be no greater than 30% of the gross profit of the business, that is a business with a gross profit to sales of 40% cannot afford to pay more than 12% (that is 30% of 40%) by way of occupancy cost.

HOW TO CALCULATE THE OCCUPANCY COST RATIO

$$\frac{\text{Total rent} + \text{all outgoings} + \text{promotion or marketing levy}}{\text{sales}}$$

What does this ratio mean when you compare it to your business' own performance and industry standards?

If the percentage is too high: This means that your business cannot afford the rental and that you would have to seriously consider seeking premises in a lower cost area. This could lead to your loss of goodwill built up because of your trading in that location for several years.

If the percentage is too low: You probably signed a lease at the bottom of the leasing cost cycle and now the landlord will be looking to a substantial increase in rental at the earliest opportunity.

4. *THE RETURN ON ASSETS RATIO*

This ratio is used to reflect the profit earning performance of your firm's assets.

It measures the efficiency of the total assets of your business in generating net profit.

It is important to note that a retailer's fit out cost must be amortized over the term of the lease, which is usually 5 years. Sufficient profit must be generated to amortize the asset as well, or it will have very little value at the end of the lease.

HOW TO CALCULATE THE RETURN ON ASSETS RATIO:

Net Profit Pre-Tax
Total Assets

What does this ratio mean when you compare it to your business' own performance and industry standards?

If the percentage is too low: A decline in the return on investment will occur if expenses rise faster than sales revenue. Therefore, this ratio should always be examined in conjunction with the gross and net profit margins. A decline may also occur if the asset base increases at a faster rate than the net profit. If you find this happening it could mean a decline in stock turn.

5. *THE STOCK TURNOVER RATIO*

This ratio measures the rate at which stock is being used on an annual basis.

For example, a stock turnover of 6, means that the average dollar volume of stock is used up almost 6 times during a financial year. It may also mean that you are turning over your stock and earning profits on that very stock every 2 months.

HOW TO CALCULATE THE STOCK TURNOVER RATIO:

$$\frac{\text{Cost of goods sold}}{\text{Stock at year end}}$$

What does this ratio mean when you compare it to your business' own performance and industry standards?

If it is too high: This may show that you have too little stock on hand to risk taking up special buys.

If it is too low: This may indicate excessive stock holding. It is necessary that you always have fresh stock on hand, or your regular customers may turn away from your store.

6. STOCK TURN DAYS

This ratio converts the stock turnover ratio calculated previously into an average stock on hand figure. For example, a stock turn day figure of 60 days means that your business keeps an average of 60 days of stock on hand during the year.

HOW TO CALCULATE THE NUMBER OF STOCK TURN DAYS

$$\frac{365}{\text{Stock turnover times}}$$

What does this ratio mean when you compare it to your business' own performance and industry standards?

If it is too high: This may indicate inadequate stock on hand or lack of risk to take up special buys.

If it is too low: This may indicate excessive stock holding. If this is the situation your goods may go out of fashion quickly or you may not have enough fresh stock on hand and your regular customers may go elsewhere.

The following example illustrates how to use the last two ratios and at the same time to compare your performance with industry standards.

Example:

If your sales for the year are $1200000 and your cost of sales are $840000, your store makes a gross profit of $360000. Given your closing stock of $140000, then the calculation is expressed as follows:

Sales	$1,200,000
Cost of sales	840,000
Gross Profit	360,000
Closing Stock	140,000

Stock turn as per the formula is thus

$$\frac{840,000}{140,000} = 6 \text{ turns}$$

Assume the industry standard for your retail category is 6.8 times.

$$\text{Your Business} = \frac{365}{6 \text{ stock turns}} = 60 \text{ days}$$

$$\text{Industry} = \frac{365}{6.8 \text{ stock turns}} = 54 \text{ days}$$

Does 6 days make such a difference to your business? Well, let us convert those days to dollars to find out using simple mathematics.

$$\text{Since:} = \frac{\text{Cost of Goods Sold}}{\text{Stock on hand}} = \text{Stock turnover}$$

$$\text{Then:} = \frac{\text{Cost of Goods Sold}}{\text{Stock on turnover}} = \text{Stock on hand}$$

And: = $$\frac{\text{Cost of Goods Sold}}{\text{Target stock turn}}$$ = Target Stock

In this case, if the industry standard is 6.8 times and your business is in line with the industry, using the above formula you will have the following:

:   = $$\frac{\text{Cost of Goods Sold}}{\text{Target stock turn}}$$ = Target Stock

-    = $$\frac{840,000}{6.8 \text{ times}}$$ = \$123,500 target stock on hand

This calculation tells you that you are holding \$16,500 too much stock (\$140,000 - \$123,500). If you divide this amount by the 6 days difference, as calculated, it tells you that one day of stock turn is worth \$2,750 in cash flow. If the stock had not been sitting there it would have been turned into cash.

Ask yourself if your banker, who has the industry standards available, would be willing to lend money to subsidise your inefficiency? I doubt it especially in these difficult times.

Once you have decided which ratio or ratios will contribute to your business, consider the following:

Structure the information so you can see relationships.

- Calculate the financial ratios.
- Record your industry benchmarks if available.
- Compare your results with industry benchmarks.
- Analyse if possible, the cause of the problems.
- Act by formulating a plan, implementing it and monitoring the results.

THE IMPORTANCE OF THE WORKING CAPITAL CYCLE

It is worthwhile noting that a second business cycle is also used by many bankers in Australia in assessing the health of the business. This is known as the working capital cycle that operates within the balance sheet.

This cycle measures the relationship between cash, inventory, and accounts receivable, and the speed and efficiency in which accounts receivable and inventory can be turned back into cash.

Most retailers do not have outstanding debtors as they usually work with credit or debit cards, but the principle remains the same.

Managing the cycle more efficiently is critical for the owner of the business and the faster the circle turns, the more cash it will generate and the lower the bank loans that will be needed to supplement the working capital of the business.

Bankers often refer to this cycle as "the survival cycle". They need to know what sucks cash out of this cycle to pay for such items as fixed asset replacements.

Remember that long-term assets should be financed by long term liabilities. Using working capital which is an asset that turns over within every 12 months should not be used to pay for new fixed assets.

CHAPTER 9

OWNING THE PROPERTY IN WHICH YOU OPERATE YOUR BUSINESS AND MAKING IT WORK FOR YOU IN TOUGH TIMES

The rent that you pay determines the value of the property to a landlord. This rent is then capitalised by a valuer at a percentage. It then becomes the yield that an investor would expect to receive from that property.

The yields range from 6% for a large shopping centre to 13% for smaller properties, depending on their location.

Example:

The property that you own and from which you trade has a capitalisation value of 10%. If you pay yourself a notional $50,000 per annum in rent, then the value of the property is expressed in the following equation:

$$\frac{\$50,000}{10\%}$$ (This is how property valuers and property owners would express this equation)

= $ 500,000

Against such a valuation, a bank may be willing to advance you 75% by way of a mortgage. You would then be in a situation to borrow 75% of $500,000 and acquire another property or invest the funds in your business.

You now have a valuable asset that you can underpin by entering a lease between yourself and an entity owning the property. You are now in a position where you can raise extra capital if you need it.

If your business can afford it, you can raise the rental and increase the capital value of the property. This is a method of using the lease effectively to improve the value of your assets.

CHAPTER 10

"OPEN TO BUY" TO CONTROL YOUR BUYING AND MANAGING YOUR STOCK LEVELS

Let us view the following situation:

1. After the Christmas sales you find that you have not made the expected and hoped for turnover.
2. You find that you are overstocked, that discounting has not had the desired effect and that you need to place new orders.

What do you do?

Having too much stock at the start of the year and not being able to move it is a problem that many retailers face at present.

A useful technique to help a retailer solve this problem is the introduction of an ***"open to buy system"*** whereby you can control your buying, particularly for some key departments in your business.

Why do you need an open to buy system in your business?

Open to Buy systems have been used by major retailers throughout Australia for many years in order to:

- control their buying
- ensure that investments in stock do not exceed their budgeted holding amounts.

- The overbuying of stock can result in the need for markdowns to reduce stock to manageable levels at the end of a season. However, this can have a drastic effect on the profitability of a business.

Can this management technique work for your business?

You may ask yourself why you need this technique, if your relationship with your supplier is so good that you can simply phone through an order and it is delivered to you immediately. Pharmacists are in this position with most medical supplies.

So, why should you change?

The reason is quite simple. As more and more new departments are introduced into retail businesses such as pharmacies, we find that some suppliers to retailers require orders to be placed a number of months in advance. Some examples include, health, shoes, vitamins and gifts for Christmas. In addition, orders for products for coughs and colds that are seasonable in nature, also have to be placed well in advance.

When retailers in toy shops or fashion retailers plan their trips to Sydney, Melbourne and other major cities for their industry fairs, to make their major purchases for the year, one of the most critical decisions is how much can they or should spend?

Therefore, when you make these important decisions, it is necessary to ensure the following:

- That purchases are made from suppliers in good time.
- That the purchases are within the cash flow of your business.

A proper open to buy system will give you the control that you need.

It is critical to the profitability of the retailer to work within these limits and thus avoid the fatal end of season markdowns.

Remember that every time you buy merchandise at an industry fair, there is pressure from industry representatives for you to buy even more. If you buy more than you can sell, even if you order the right items, where will you get the money to pay your bills?

The answer is proper purchases planning ahead and to have an open-to-buy plan which will ensure that markdowns do not happen.

This plan will ensure that the flow of merchandise into your store will be able to support anticipated sales at the desired stock turn rates and give you a positive cash flow.

> **TIP**
>
> Traditional inventory control or accounting systems will not provide you with this important projected information, yet it is one of the most effective cash flow and stock management systems available to you.

It is not hard to set up an open to buy plan. Retailers familiar with the use of a personal computer and spread sheet will be able to prepare one easily.

HOW TO ACHIEVE YOUR PLANNED OBJECTIVES?

To achieve your objectives, it is critical for your purchases to be planned in light of the following: -

- Bearing in mind your current stock levels at the start of the season.
- Looking at the level of stock you wish to have on hand at the end of the season.
- Looking at the budgeted levels of sales you need per month.
- Assessing the number of times you turn over our stock in a season.
- Being aware of the number of purchases you have committed yourself to at any point of time.

All the above ingredients are added into your open to buy plan

OPEN TO BUY PLAN

How then does this plan operate?

The objective of the plan is to enforce a discipline on the retailer that only allows future purchases to come in at the end of the season, if they are in line with the PLANNED CLOSING LEVEL OF STOCK that was set at the start of the season.

This plan is obviously not set in concrete and will change as the season progresses.

For example, if sales achievements are exceeding budgets in a particular month, the open to buy plan during the balance of the season wil have to be increased, otherwise stocks will be deleted and sales targets in later months will not be achieved.

Remember that the intention of this plan is for the closing stock to remain unchanged.

Do you keep your open to buy plan at cost or at retail?

Some retailers maintain their open to buy plans at retail others prefer to keep them at cost. Both have advantages and disadvantages. I recommend that it is simpler keep it at cost.

KEEPING THE PLAN AT COST

For simplicity purposes, most retailers maintain their stocks and purchase orders at cost. All you need to do to maintain the open to buy at cost is to reduce *budgeted sales* to *cost of sales* by applying the *budgeted gross profit*.

So, before we continue with the steps necessary to formulate the open to buy plan, let us look at an example of the sales budget for the next six months and apply this calculation to reduce it to cost.

CALCULATION TO REDUCE COST OF SALES

From your sales budgets, calculate what your cost of sales will be in each month and enter these in the cost of sales line for the season.

If sales is 100% (A) and the Gross Profit is anticipated to be 40% (B)

then Cost of Sales will be A- B = 60%

LET'S LOOK AT AN EXAMPLE OF A SALES BUDGET FOR 2021/22 AND APPLY THE ABOVE FORMULA

SALES BUDGET SUMMER 2021/22

	Budget Sales 100%	Gross Profit 40%	Cost of Sales 60%
Sept	2167	867	1300
Oct	1833	733	1100
Nov	1917	767	1150
Dec	2833	1133	1700
Jan	1167	467	700
Feb	917	367	550

THE FORMULA FOR CALCULATING AN OPEN TO BUY PLAN

The formula for calculating your open to buy on your spread sheet will always be as follows:

> **Closing stock budget at cost + sales budget for month at cost - opening stock at cost - goods on order due in the month at cost**
>
> **= *Open to Buy for the Month at Cost***

Example:

This example shows more clearly how the plan works. You will understand more about using a spread sheet for your calculations by looking at the annexure at the end of this section of the book .

Month of September

Closing stock Budget at 30 September	2250
Plus: Sales Budget at cost	1300
	3550
Less: Opening stock at 1 September at cost	1000
	2550
Less: Goods on order due in September at cost	2400

Open to Buy at Cost 150.

Continuing with the previous example. If for instance, your budgeted sales at cost for October are $1100 and costs for November $1150, based on a two-month stock holding, it is then prudent to ensure that you have stock on hand by the end of September of $2250.

Some questions often asked by retailers about open to buy programs are as follows:

How long in advance should an open to buy program be calculated?

It should be calculated some months prior to use, particularly where seasonable buying takes place as in the Christmas season where buying of gifts starts early.

It is always wise to have your open to buy programme in place before you go to the trade fair.

Should I always buy to the full amount of my open to buy?

From a strategic perspective, it is advisable *not* to buy to the full value of your open to buy plan. Rather allow yourself a percentage of about 10 % to take advantage of special deals or purchases of new items. You can even replace stock that sells out quicker than anticipated.

How do I go about setting the stock levels that I wish to hold at month ends and at the end of the season?

This is determined by the normal annual stock turn of your business. Assume you have a stock-turn of six times a year based on your previous results. This means that you are turning your stock over every two months.

It is then essential to have on hand or in transit, stock to at least the next two months cost of sales value, or you could run out of your stock and you could lose out on sales.

AN EXAMPLE USING YOUR SPREADSHEET

Now using your spread sheet let's put all the information together and set up an open to buy plan.

Remember that this is merely a guide and that you will have to add and change seasonal factors such as Christmas Sales and Black Friday Sales, and Spot Sales, in your calculations.

Step 1

You have made the decision that you wish to end the season at the end of February with the same level of stock as the opening stock at beginning of September, namely 1000.

Using your spread sheet enter 1000 as your opening stock in September 2011 and 1000 as your closing stock at the end of February 2012. *This closing stock figure cannot change.*

Step 2

Now let's look at the on-order line, and add each month the goods you have already ordered from suppliers as well as forward charging and possibly proposed orders from the fair.

The figures in this example are as follows.

Sept	2400
Oct	1800
Nov	850
Dec	600
Jan	500
Feb	450

Now fill this in under the appropriate month on the spread sheet.

Step 3

From your previous calculation now inset the cost of sales for each month.

Step 4

On the basis that you turn your stock over six times per annum, it will be necessary to regard the next two month's cost of sales as the closing stock. As seen previously, because you propose a cost of sales of $1100 in October and $1150 in November, your budgeted stock at the end of September should be $2250.

Enter this figure and complete the remainder of the row on your spread sheet.

Step 5

With the exception of the closing stock at the end of February 2022 which is fixed, you can complete the closing month's stock levels in the spread sheet for all the intervening months.

Step 6

- Using the formula you can now complete the missing figures in September - . namely opening stock of $1000 plus on order of $2400. This gives a sub total of $3400 available for sale during the month.
- From this sub-total you can deduct the cost of sales for the month of $1300 to give you a sub-total of $2100 (your theoretical stock on hand).
- However, you have calculated that to meet the next two months sales, your stock on hand should have been $2250.
- Therefore, you now deduct this budgeted stock from your sub- total. When you look at your new sub-total, you will find that your targeted stock is short by $150 to meet your targeted stock level.

You thus have open to buy of $150.

If your purchases for the month of September are increased to:

$2400 + $150 = $2550, then your actual stock at the end of the September will equal your theoretical stock. This is then the stock you need to hold in order to meet the cost of the next two months sales.

Step 7

The budgeted closing stock of $2250 at the end of September now becomes the opening stock at the beginning of October and so on.

You can now re-arrange the formula provided that you have placed no further orders prior to the fair, and that you propose to order all your stock at the fair. Or you can create a purchasing budget to link to your proposed cost of sales.

The formula is now as follows.:

> **Purchases for month = Closing stock + cost of sales - opening stock**

You can now place your purchase orders in the exact month required to achieve the sales levels that you have budgeted for and finish up with the level of stock that you planned for.

It goes without saying, that the level of purchases will depend on the level of sales that are achieved in your store during the season.

If your trend of sales decreases, do not be afraid to cancel orders to keep your buying in line. If you do not, you may not achieve the level of stock that you have set yourself to close with at the end of the season.

In this way, at the end of each month you will be able to amend the spread sheet with your actual stock on hand and with new projected sales figures. This provides you with a revised open to buy. It may mean that you have to cancel orders or bring orders forward, but at least *you will have a plan and you will know what to do.*

TIP

There is nothing worse than attempting to estimate your stock needs by pure gut feeling.

I can recommend this plan to all retailers who have had problems in the past with ordering. This programme works best when the entire retail team is involved in buying for the store and are committed to the plan and the discipline that it requires. You will feel the benefits of using it very quickly.

CHAPTER 11

REQUESTING AND NEGOTIATING A RENTAL REBATE FROM A LANDLORD IN DIFFICULT TRADING CONDITIONS

As the economic recession deepens, to simply survive, more retailers are in desperate need of some rental relief from their landlords. I believe that retailers should never be afraid to ask for a rental abatement. You will find that landlords do not wish to lose a good tenant.

The task is often left to the retailer to start the negotiations by preparing a letter requesting rent relief and a meeting with the landlord. A typical letter requesting a rebate from a landlord would be along the following lines:

The Landlord
ABC Shopping Centre
Dear Sir

Re: Lease of XYZ Pty Ltd at the ABC Shopping Centre.

As you are aware, retail trading conditions in Australia have deteriorated substantially since the start of this financial year, with most retailers experiencing lower sales and reduced margins. Our category of retail sales is no exception.

Our performance at the above centre has now reached a level where our

Board of Directors has requested me to seek some form of rental abatement from you to assist us in the short term, until retail conditions improve.

We are thus proposing the following for your consideration:

1. That we be provided with a rental abatement of $xxxx per month either by way of a credit on our rental statement or by way of an advertising concession. This abatement is to be for a period of 6 months to 31 December 2022 when it can be reviewed.
2. We will continue to pay our share of outgoings and marketing levy as per the lease.
3. Any rental increases as per the lease due prior will be waived and forgiven.

Looking forward to a favourable response to the above request.

Yours faithfully

If you receive an outright "no" from the landlord, you may have a real problem especially if you have been well in arrears with your rent payments or not paid your rent on time, the landlord may not worry about your leaving the centre.

If the landlord has agreed to meet with you to discuss the situation, you need to prepare your case very carefully as you are likely to have only one go at explaining why you need rent relief.

PUTTING UP YOUR CASE

1. You need to have all the necessary information with you at the meeting to justify the rent reduction and be willing to share it with the landlord.
2. Have your accountant prepare a current, accurate set of financials.
3. If you are in a shopping centre, ascertain the number of retailers in your category when you started the lease and the current number.
4. Ascertain if possible, the impact of online sales in your category and how this is affecting your business.
5. From statistical data available, determine the trend of traffic flow to the centre for the last few years, and whether this has been in decline or not.

6. Demonstrate that you have tried to execute all alternative strategies to improve sustainability.
7. Show that you have a plan of action as to how you will leverage the possible rent relief. For example, a local advertising campaign to bring more customers to your store and to the centre.
8. If your rent is currently in arrears, show how you propose to pay it back. You may even consider using the bond money which the landlord holds to be offset against the arrears.
9. It is important to make the landlord feel that you are both in partnership in the business and that you both need to share the risk in the current climate.

No one knows how long the retail downturn will continue, so ask for your rent relief in say 6 monthly periods with the situation reviewed at the end of each period.

Be creative in how the rent relief is paid to you. For example, it may be more tax effective or more valuable for the landlord to give you an advertising allowance in lieu of rent relief, which in addition to this allowance being tax deductible, also maintains the rental income for valuation purposes.

CHAPTER 12

MEASURING THE VALUE YOU RECEIVE FOR YOUR ADVERTISING AND CATALOGUE DOLLAR

One of the major expenses that most retailers usually reduce in a downturn is advertising. However, you cannot stop advertising altogether as the public will soon forget about you. The secret is to spend your advertising dollar to its best advantage.

Many retailers post Covid-19 have concentrated on promoting and advertising their websites.

Firstly, let us look how retailers usually plan their advertising spend so that you can choose the one that suits your needs.

A. BUDGETING FOR ADVERTISING

There are about five major budgeting techniques used by retailers and buying associations today in determining their advertising and promotional budgets:

1. ALL YOU CAN AFFORD PROCEDURE

- This is the weakest of the budgeting methods.
- All other retailing costs are accounted for and what is over is placed in your advertising budget.
- Little importance is placed on advertising as a retail mix variable.

- Expenditure is not linked to objectives.
- It is a form of no funds no advertising.
- It is a method used predominantly by small conservative retailers.

2. ARBITRARY OR HISTORICAL METHOD

- This method relies on previous budgets. A percentage is added or subtracted from this year's budget to determine next year's budget.
- This is a technique useful for small operators.
- It is an easy method to calculate.
- A reference point is therefore used as a measurement.
- The budget is adjusted based on your feelings about past success and future trends.
- The disadvantage is that size of the budget is rarely tied to specific objectives and evaluations are difficult.

3. THE COMPETITIVE PARITY METHOD

- The advertising budget is raised or lowered according to the actions of competitors. If a leading retailer in an area raises his advertising by 8%, competitors in the area follow suit.
- It is often used by small and large retailers.
- The advantage is that it provides a point of comparison and is market-orientated.
- The disadvantages are that you are following and not leading.
- It can be difficult to obtain data, and so assumptions of similarities in businesses, years in business, size, location, pricing policy and buying group membership must be made.

4. PERCENTAGE - ON- SALES TECHNIQUE

- The retailer basis the advertising budget on sales revenue.
- In past years, the retailer established an advertising- to- sales ratio of about 3% of sales. In future years, the ratio will remain constant and the amount to be spent on advertising will vary according to the planned sales for the year.
- The benefits are the use of sales as a base for comparison.
- The shortcomings are that there is no relation to objectives. For an

established retailer, an increase in sales may not require an increase in advertising. The advertising dollar spent tends to decrease during poor sales periods, when in fact an advertising boost could be beneficial to sales.

- This technique usually results in too much advertising in periods of high sales and too little advertising in periods of low sales.

5. THE OBJECTIVE TASK METHOD

- With this method, the retailer clearly defines his advertising objectives and then determines the size of the budget necessary to satisfy these objectives.
- The number of goals that can be achieved in a year is only limited by the cash resources of the business.
- The advantage is that goals are clearly stated. For example, the cost to establish greater awareness of the store name is decided in advance.
- Expenditure on advertising is related to the completion of goal orientated tasks. Therefore, the method is adaptable and success or failure can be evaluated.
- The major shortcoming is the complexity in setting goals, especially for small retailers.

In determining which of these combinations of techniques you decide to use, you must weigh up the strengths and weaknesses in relation to your individual requirements and constraints. The percentage on sales technique is the most popular method with retailers in Australia.

PLANNING FOR ADVERTISING

Planning an advertising budget means that you need to think carefully about what results you expect from your advertising. Ask yourself:

- How much money is available for advertising?
- Are you looking for an increase in total sales?
- Are you interested in more sales of a particular product line?
- Are you trying to defend yourself against a competitor?
- If you do not advertise will people still remember that your busines exist?

> **TIP**
>
> Remember, that all the best advertising techniques and objectives in the world are of little value if your store is untidy, your staff is not properly trained to deal with customers and the ambiance of your store does not reflect what you are trying to convey in your advertising message, online website or catalogue. You must get your house in order before you invite visitors to buy your goods.

HOW TO CALCULATE YOUR ADVERTISING BUDGET

For your advertising dollar to be well spent and achieve its objective in future sales you must look carefully at your products and decide on how much of your advertising dollar to allocate to each. Look at the following example:

Example:

Assume your sales budget for next month is $50000 and you basically have 5 product groupings in your store:

Product	Sales Target $	% of total sales
1	5000	10
2	20000	40
3	10000	20
4	5000	10
5	10000	20
	50000	100

Assume we are adopting the percentage on sales method and have allocated 5 % of forecasted sales. That is $2500.

First look at how much you want to allocate to the budget to achieve your objectives.

Then you allocate the advertising budget to each product line according to its percentage of forecasted sales, that have been adjusted to reflect the specific objectives for the month.

Your objectives for the Month:

1. Products in groups 1 and 5 require normal advertising.
2. Products in group 2 attract co-operative advertising from the manufacturer.
3. You are trying to expand sales of products in group 3.
4. You need to clear excessive stocks of products in group 4.

Allocation of the advertising dollars for the month per product group is thus as follows:

Product line objectives	% of sales	% of advertising	Product line advertising $
1 - normal	10	10	250
2 - plus co-op	40	20	500
3 - expand	20	30	750
4 - overstocked	10	20	500
5 - normal	20	20	500
	100	100	2500

Many retailers keep a monthly advertising calendar to complete their advertising budget. The calendar should have enough space to record the advertising media planned for each day, the major theme, notes on featured products and most importantly, the cost.

Many retailers also keep information such as sales from the previous year, the number of transactions on a particular day and the theme of last year's advertisements, to help them decide on how to spend their advertising dollar.

Having determined the days of the month that will produce the best results, the best advertising medium for your objectives and the products you want to promote, you will have created a powerful advertising strategy which will maximise the effectiveness of your advertising budget.

USE OF CATALOGUES FOR ADVERTISING

Example:

A pharmacy buying group, that services the advertising requirements of a diverse number of pharmacists and geographic locations in Australia, finds that catalogues are their best form of advertising and forms the key to their advertising campaigns.

These catalogues are produced 7 or 8 times a year at specific selling times.

The products to be included in each catalogue are selected by a special committee of members.

Where possible, they try to include in their catalogues " shut out" products, that from experience in the past gave members the best gross margins.

The catalogues cost about 7 cents each to produce and members of their group can purchase as many as they require to service their area.

As a rule of thumb, sales from catalogues account for about 30 % of sales

EVALUATING THE PERFORMANCE OF A CATALOGUE

To assess whether you are receiving value for your advertising dollar, from a catalogue, you must always prepare a profit and loss statement for each catalogue to determine its viability as follows:

Example:

Advertising for a single product retailer		
Sales of product advertised in two weeks prior to catalogue		$500
Sales of product advertised in 2 weeks while catalogue in customers home		$1250
Increase in sales directly attributable to catalogue		$750
Selling price per product		$100
Gross profit per product normal - 50%		$ 50
Gross profit allowed for in catalogue - 30 %		$30

Profit and loss from Christmas Catalogue		
Extra profit generated from catalogue	750 x $30	= $22500
Less Cost of catalogue		
Production 100000 x 7cents	$7000	
Distribution costs	$10000	
		= $17000
Extra gross profit generated		$ 5500

In this example, the catalogue was cost effective yielding extra gross profit of $5500.

TIP

Remember, that as well as the measured value of the catalogue, in the minds of your customers you are reinforcing your name, and your location. You may have an online website as well.

Always spend according to your cash budget but do not stop spending on advertising.

CHAPTER 13

MANAGING YOUR CASH FLOW

To survive the squeeze in today's retail climate, cash is king.

Small businesses are especially vulnerable to cash flow problems. Many tend to operate with inadequate reserves. The withdrawal of the "shopkeeper allowance" has increased the problem. Because small businesses don't put themselves through the discipline of preparing their cash flow statements on a regular basis, they tend to miss the signs of a cash flow deficit until it is too late. Then they find that the stress multiplies. Do not allow yourself to fall in this position.

Timing and cash flow are inseparable. Given the seasonal fluctuations experienced in most small retail businesses with the matching of the timing of cash inflows and cash outflows, it's not easy for the small business person to function without proper cash flow projections. Therefore planning is necessary.

If the cash flow <u>into</u> your business *EXCEEDS* the cash flow <u>out</u> of your business, you can continue to operate and survive. However, if the trend reverses and your business runs out of cash, you will soon grind to a halt.

Remember, that even if you have a cash shortfall for a short time and you have not notified your bank well in advance, they may lose faith in your business and in today's tough business environment *"pull the plug"* on you.

The introduction of GST has had a severe impact on cash flows. It was intended to give businesses a cash flow boost as they would collect the GST and use the funds until the GST had to be paid over. However, it is not often used in the way it was intended.

WHAT IS THE DIFFERENCE BETWEEN A PROFIT AND LOSS STATEMENT AND A CASH FLOW STATEMENT?

Many small business operators are confused between a "profit and loss statement" and a "cash flow statement". Both use your business's identical arithmetical numbers, but crunch them in different ways for different purposes.

A. PROFIT AND LOSS STATEMENT

The profit and loss account, which we will look at shortly, shows how you are using your resources to produce sales.

When examining a profit and loss statement you normally look at 4 items – sales, cost of goods sold, total operating expenses and net profit.

Unless there is a major change in the business operation, these numbers should remain stable from month to month. If the numbers are not stable, you need to find out why. You may be over-spending, missing discounts, or perhaps you are missing the opportunity to cut costs on a regular basis.

B. CASH FLOW STATEMENT

Every business plans to make a profit each year. However, you need to know *how cash comes in and goes out of your business*. Cash flow analysis provides the means for you to conduct a periodic check on the financial health of your business.

Preparing a projected cash flow statement, estimates the stream of money that will be coming into the business during the months to come, based on a history of your sales and expenses. The cash flow statement then becomes the core tool for maintaining your control over your business' finances.

Remember, you can show a profit, but still be short on cash if a large customer is late in paying.

Like the profit and loss statement, the cash flow statement should be produced monthly. If this is not possible, you should at least do full quarterly profit and loss and cash flow statements to coincide with the preparation of your BAS return.

To survive, you need to constantly know:

- *Where the money is in your business.*
- *Where is the money going?*
- *And how can you get more and when you need it?*

Your bank overdraft facilities are there to tide you over the fluctuations within the quarter. A positive cash flow gives you the forward motion to build and grow your business.

A CASH FLOW STATEMENT CAN ALSO TELL YOU ABOUT THE HEALTH OF YOUR BUSINESS

It is a waste of time preparing a forward cash flow statement if at the end of the month you do not compare your actual cash flow performance with your projected cash flow performance. Even a small lag in sales can have a dramatic impact on your cash flow, but you may not know about it if you don't prepare a projected cash flow statement and review it at month end.

Your comparisons between actual and budget may be far out of line because you failed to see, for example, additional casual staff needs over Christmas. Perhaps you missed a major jump in prices from suppliers, or even the devaluation of the Australian dollar when your letters of credit on imports were due. **Do not panic**! Cut back on cash outflows, delay payments where possible, ask your suppliers for more time but, more importantly:

Learn the lesson that you must prepare cash flow statements that more realistically meet your needs so that they do not throw up surprises next time.

HOW THEN DO YOU KEEP YOUR CASH FLOW UNDER CONTROL?

There are four steps to proper cash flow planning:

1. FORECAST YOUR INCOME FROM SALES

This forecast is the most important step in cash flow planning. It is your best estimate of your sales split up by month.

It is usually done by taking your last year's sales and adding a percentage. You can then estimate the number of sales you are likely to make multiplied by the average selling price per transaction. This will translate into dollar volume of sales. If you honestly believe that sales will fall because of the retail climate, bite the bullet and make sure that you provide for lower sales in your cash budget.

Since retailers and hospitality businesses mainly sell for cash or on credit cards, your cash inflow from sales will be the same as your sales forecast. If you have some accounts on credit you must then estimate how collections will be made from these accounts.

2. IDENTIFY CASH OUTFLOWS:

In every business there are expenses that occur on a regular basis.

Items such as salaries and wages, payments to government departments arising from salary and wage payments like payroll tax, FBT, superannuation as well as normal operating expenses such as insurance and light and power costs.

Examine your rent and outgoing outflows. Ask yourself if they are in line with your leases. It is important to determine if this is the case. Also check your lease to see when you are due for a rent review. You will have to consider the extra rent. Particularly if you are in arrears because of Covid-19.

If you are registered for GST on a quarterly basis, you must pay the amounts charged on sales less your input tax credits to the tax office 21 days after each quarter.

Any advertising expenditure such as payment for catalogues or brochures can be anticipated and easily calculated, and must be in the appropriate month's expenses.

Identify in advance the cost and likely purchase date of capital expenditure items such as replacement of a car or buying a small personal computer. And include that in the appropriate month they will be paid for.

Do not forget about your deferred income tax payments for last year or pay as you go payments this year. Your accountant has probably reminded you about them. They must also be included in your statement.

This leaves the largest out flow to be identified, namely your purchases. The ratio and analysis we performed earlier shows that suppliers need to be paid within 30 days to get the maximum discounts. Let us now look at an example:

You are working on a 35% gross profit; your cost of sales will be 65% of your sales payable in arrears. This is explained in the following table:

Example:

CASH FLOW WORKSHEET TO ESTIMATE SALES, PURCHASES AND GST PAYMENTS FOR YEAR ENDED 30 JUNE 2022

Month	Last Year's Sales By Month	% of Total Sales	Sales Budget This Year	10% GST to be added	Gross Profit Of 35%	Purchases 65% of Sales	Month Paid
JULY	108,550	6.5%	121,875	12,188	42,656	79,219	AUG
AUGUST	116,900	7.0%	131,250	13,125	45,938	85,313	SEPT
SEPTEMBER	150,300	9.0%	168,750	16,875	59,063	109,688	OCT
OCTOBER	125,250	7.5%	140,625	14,063	49,219	91,406	NOV
NOVEMBER	167,000	10.0%	187,500	18,750	56,625	121,875	DEC
DECEMBER	233,900	14.0%	262,500	26,250	91,875	170,625	JAN

PART 1
FINANCIAL MANAGEMENT

JANUARY	116,900	7.0%	131,250	13,125	45,938	85,313	FEB
FEBRUARY	100,200	6.0%	112,500	11,250	39,375	73,125	MAR
MARCH	183,700	11.0%	206,250	20,625	72,188	134,063	APRIL
APRIL	141,950	8.5%	159,375	15,938	55,781	103,594	MAY
MAY	91,850	5.5%	103,125	10,313	36,094	67,031	JUNE
JUNE	133,600	8.0%	150,000	15,000	52,500	97,500	JULY
TOTAL	1,670,000	100%	1,875,000	187,500	656,250	1,218,750	

Note: The amount of purchases to be paid in July 2022 is 8% of the previous year'

3. ANALYSE THE NET EFFECT OF CASH FLOWS IN AND OUT

Simply summarise the cash flows in and out as per the example, determining when the major cash drains are likely to be and how far this is likely to take you over your bank overdraft limits.

Next, look at rescheduling your payments to" smooth out" the month end "humps".

Now you will have to make some important decisions. Should you delay new capital expenditure or approach the tax office to allow you to pay off amounts owing in instalments?

4. ARRANGE FACILITIES WITH THE BANK

Alternatively, you may have to ask the bank manager for a temporary facility for a few weeks. When you see your bank manager make sure that you can accurately forecast your possible cash defects for the months ahead. He is aware of today's tough times, and if he feels that you are in control of your business, he may be prepared to assist you.

If you have a substantial surplus over the December month end, it would be wise to invest this temporarily to meet the heavy outflow in cash for January and February.

Before you go to see your bank manager for either a temporary overdraft facility or maybe for a loan to refurbish your store as is required under your lease, there are two things you must have:

- A cash flow statement for the next 12 months.
- A business plan.

Now that we have looked at the cash flow statement we need to look at preparing a business plan.

CHAPTER 14

A TYPICAL BUSINESS PLAN FOR A RETAIL BUSINESS

In an economic downturn like during Covid19, it is essential that any business that aims to remain healthy must have a business plan, that it is revised and revised as circumstances change. Bankers, suppliers, landlords or others who provide you with credit will most likely ask you produce it before they will advance you any further funding.

To give an accurate picture of how your business operates, your business plan should contain the following points:

- An executive summary.
- A summary of the industry in which you operate.
- A description of your company and your lease arrangements with your landlord.
- An overview of your products and current marketing strategy
- Your customer profiles.
- Your competition.
- Details of the management of the business and its legal and accounting advisers.
- A staff profile
- If you are applying for a loan from your bank, you must show how the proceeds of the loan will be spent.
- A financial summary of a 5-year trend of the business to date, and how the loan will impact your balance sheet and profit and loss account.
- Any other pertinent information the bank or supplier may require

Example

The following is an example of how to prepare a typical business plan for a retail store.

SMITH'S RETAIL SHOE STORE EXECUTIVE SUMMARY

Smith's Shoes Pty Ltd is seeking a loan of $150,000. The adjacent store is to be taken over to enlarge the existing premises and they want to use the funding to purchase all fixtures and fittings for the premises to be taken over. They also intend to remove the intervening wall and refurbish the enlarged premises.

Part of the loan will be used to pay off the existing bank loan and to refinance a new loan at the lower interest rates prevailing in Australia at present. The loan will be financed by a first mortgage over the current retail premises owned by the Smith Family.

The loan will be repaid over 5 years. It is anticipated that the increased sales resulting from the larger premises will generate sufficient profits to repay it.

The industry in which you operate.

Despite the current economic climate in Australia there has been an increase in the demand for footwear sales. The Bureau of Statistics has shown a growth of about 3% over the past 12 months. The category of footwear with the highest growth has been in children's wear and back to school shoes, as well as a demand for high quality walking shoes and athletic footwear.

Due to the limiting size of the store premises, the company has been unable to keep a large enough range of these products to satisfy demand. An enlargement of the premises will allow them to do this. It is anticipated that current sales could increase by about 30% because of this expansion. With additional products, they expect to show a higher gross margin than previously even with only conventional men's and ladies' shoes.

Company description

Smith's Shoe shop is an independent shoe retail proprietary company. Though it is a single operator, it is well known in Geelong and has been established for some 35 years. The current store managers are the third generation of the Smith family who originally founded the store in 1966.

After leasing the premises for 5 years, the original founder acquired the property at 20 Stumpy Street Geelong, and it has been owned by the family ever since. The property has a mortgage on it of $60000. It was recently valued at $425000. *A copy of this valuation is attached.*

The new premises will be leased from a private landlord for a period of 5 years with two further options of 5 years each at a rental of $18000 per annum.

The existing premises were refurbished some 8 years ago, and hence the bank loan outstanding on this refurbishment. The company has repaid the bank to date nearly $80,000 of the original loan plus interest.

PRODUCT OVERVIEW AND CURRENT MARKETING STRATEGY

The stores position in the marketplace

The company operates primarily in the CBD of Geelong and services a passing traffic of about 4 million visitors to the CBD annually. Though known by its family name of Smith's Shoes it is a member of the Australian Buying Group and is thus part of the purchasing power of some 500 stores that operate under that marketing banner throughout Australia. Most of the product is sourced through ABG but some 20% is sourced from their own business connections overseas. This results in higher-than-normal gross profits.

Although based in Geelong, the company's reputation extends throughout the district. Many of the out-of-town customers visit the store at least once or twice during the year to enjoy the service and range of larger shoe sizes stocked by the company and favoured by many rural customers. These sizes are not usually kept by national operators and department stores.

The store offers both ladies and men's shoes as well as a small selection of children's and teenage shoes. It stocks a particularly good though limited range of "back to school" shoes in accordance with the requirements of many of the schools in Geelong and district. Again, these shoes are offered in larger sizes beyond that stocked by other competitors.

Customer profile

The demographic profile of Smith's shoppers is unique in that the store enjoys an equal weighting of male and female buyers with a strong bias to younger people. In addition, customers are diversified not only by ethnic origin, but also increasingly by the changing Australian family profile.

Through on the floor contact and sophisticated computerised analysis, the store can monitor the requirements of its customers and changing trends and fashions.

Competition

Smith's Competitors in Geelong can be said to fall under the following classification.

At lower retail price points:	Kmart
	Big W
	Target
	Weekend Markets
At Middle to Upper price points	Williams
	Mathers
	Wittners
	Jane Mercer
	Foot Locker

STRATEGY/TACTICS

Management of the Business

The current principals and owners of the business are William and Jeffrey Wright who are the grandchildren of the original owners. William has a business diploma from the University of Ballarat and Jeffrey, after spending a period of 8 years in the shoe manufacturing division of Pacific Dunlop, then joined his brother in the business on the death of his farther.

Both have experience in IT and have set up sophisticated computer systems in the monitoring of the company's stock control, sales analysis and buying functions. The company has a modern website for marketing its products.

The company has engaged the services of the following advisers

An Accountant

A retail consultant and lease negotiator

A Solicitor

STAFF

At the date of the preparation of this document, the company in addition to its 2 directors, employs a staff of 5 persons, of which 3 are full time and 2 part time over weekends. The 5 staff comprise 4 female shop assistants and 1 male shop assistant.

It is the intention to engage I full time person and 2 part time persons to staff the extra floor space arising out of the enlarged premises. Jeffery Wright is responsible for hiring, training, and supervising the staff. The company is undergoing an intense retail training program which has greatly enhanced the staff's selling techniques, add on selling and visual merchandising. It has also installed an online buying website which has improved its ecommerce sales.

The new staff will also to be involved in the training program. They are all on incentive programs to generate sales and to sell shoes at higher price points than advertised lines.

FINANCIAL DATA:

Application and use of new funds to be raised

The proceeds of the proposed $250,000 loan will be used as follows:

Repayment of Current Loan	$60,000
Fixtures and fittings	$55,000
Additional Working Capital	$135,000
	$250,000

The additional working capital will be invested in stock and staff as well as an advertising campaign on radio to advertise the newly enlarged departments at the store.

Let us now look at an example that will demonstrate how to draw up financial forecasts and projections in this example of a retail store:

THE FINANCIAL FORECASTS AND PROJECTIONS FOR SMITH'S SHOE STORE

FIVE YEAR SALES AND PROFIT TREND TO 30 JUNE 2022

	2018	2019	2020	2021	2022
SALES:	770000	845000	887000	928000	975000
GROSS PROFIT:	40.9	39.9	40.6	40.1	41.1
NET PROFIT PRE-TAX:	62005	65030	68809	79804	71787
STOCKTURN:	3.7	3.7	3.8	3.9	4.0

COMBINED BALANCE SHEET AT 30 JUNE 2022

	BEFORE FINANCING			AFTER FINANCING
	PROP CO	TRADING CO	CONSOLIDTD	CONSOLIDTD
ASSETS				
Cash	0	32000	32000	67000
Accounts Receivable	0	33000	33000	33000
Prepaid	0	18000	18000	18000
Stock	0	169000	169000	169000
Total Current Assets	0	252000	252000	287000
Property	450000	0	450000	450000
Motor Vehicles	0	22000	22000	22000
Fixtures and Fittings	0	128000	128000	183000
Office Equip	0	83600	83600	83600
Total Fixed Assets	450000	233600	683600	738600
Total Assets	450000	485600	935600	1025600

	BEFORE FINANCING			AFTER FINANCING
	PROP CO	TRADING CO	CONSOLIDTD	CONSOLIDTD
LIABILITIES & NET WORTH				
Bank Overdraft	0	28050	28050	28050
Accounts Payable	0	84000	84000	84000
Accruals	0	2100	2100	2100
GST/Group tax/Payg	35000	38500	73500	73500
Provisions	0	4100	4100	4100
14 Total Current Liabilities	35000	156750	191750	191750
Loans	60000	0	60000	150000
Total Long Term Liabilities	60000	0	60000	150000
Total Liabilities	95000	156750	251750	341750
Share Capital	80000	100000	180000	180000
Retained Earnings	155000	168850	323850	323850
Capital Reserve Prop revaluation	180000	0	180000	180000
Net Worth	415000	268850	683850	683850
Total Liabilities and Net Worth	510000	425600	935600	1025600

Current Ratio = current assets   **287000** = **1.5 : 1**
                     current liabilities   **191750**

INCOME STATEMENT FOR THE 5 YEARS ENDED 30 JUNE 2022

	2018	2019	2020	2021	2022
Sales	975000	1200000	1350000	1450000	1500000
Cost of Goods Sold	574763	684000	769500	826500	855000
Gross Profit	400237	516000	580500	623500	645000
% Gross Profit/Sales	41.05	43.00	43.00	43.00	43.00
Less: Operating Expenses					
Salaries & Wages	127600	147600	154425	158800	163800
Salary & Wages Oncosts	18500	20000	21000	22500	23000
Occupancy Costs	60000	78000	80000	82000	84000
Advertising	16300	18500	19000	20000	20000

Energy Costs	23580	31000	32400	33500	34000
Motor Expenses	25000	26000	27000	28000	28500
Insurance	19750	22000	22800	23800	24000
Bad Debts	3200	3500	3500	3500	3500
Depreciation	26800	31000	31000	31000	31000
Audit and Accounting	1820	2000	2000	2000	2500
Other Store Expenses	9200	12000	12500	13000	14000
Interest Paid	4000	7000	6525	6200	5800
Total Expenses	335750	398600	412150	424300	434100
Operating Profit	64487	117400	168350	199200	210900
Disc Recd & Other Income	7300	8000	9000	10000	10000
Net Profit Pre Tax	71787	125400	177350	209200	220900
Tax	21536	37620	53205	62760	66270
Net Profit After Tax	50251	87780	124145	146440	154630
% net profit pre tax to sales	7.36	10.45	13.14	14.43	14.73
break even sales	817905	926977	958488	986744	1009535

A final note

Now that you have read this example, have another look at your business plan and try to make it clear and concise without leaving out all the important points about your business functions, management, financials, and position in the marketplace.

CHAPTER 15

HOW TO INTERACT AND COMMUNICATE WITH YOUR BANK MANAGER

Armed with a cash flow forecast and business plan as well as the knowledge of any commercial tenancy relief scheme issued by states at the time of Coivid-19, it is now time to approach your bank manager.

There are many rumours about banks not wishing to make loans to retailers for refurbishments. Naturally, this might make you anxious about approaching your bank manager regarding a loan to refurbish your store or for a temporary cash flow facility.

Visiting a bank manager can for some seem as unpleasant as visiting the dentist. But it does not have to hurt. When you visit him, you might expect to be grilled on every aspect of the running of your business and see yourself virtually begging for that extra cash to tide you through. After all, it is his job to protect the bank from a loan that may never be repaid. But it does not have to hurt - at least not as much as you think.

Remember, that bankers will evaluate you based on your personal and business credibility. The stronger your credit rating the better the terms, interest rates and bank charges you will be able to negotiate.

A bank makes its assessment on granting a business loan on 2 factors- the assets a tenant can offer as security and the reliability and business skills of the management.

From experience in dealing with bankers over several years and trying to raise loans, these are some ideas to assist you:

- As well as financial data to back up your request for a loan, provide your bank manager with a simple and clear presentation with graphs and photos where necessary, so that he can fully understand your situation. His staff will then take the time to carefully scrutinise your figures.
- A person who is well prepared with exact figures and working knowledge of current conditions will have a better chance than someone who doesn't. Bankers like confident people and exact numbers, not guesses or estimates.
- Think it through and try to anticipate the questions that you will be asked and plan your responses.
- Never give the impression that you are desperate for help. Bankers prefer to loan money to people who do not have to borrow. If you do not ask for any concessions and you just sit there, you make a banker nervous. You look too hungry.
- Refuse to allow yourself to be intimidated. Many entrepreneurs carry a false perception that negotiating for a better deal or a lower interest rate may anger the banker and could lead to a denial. Quite the contrary.
- Negotiating strongly with understanding and a frugal attitude to your business will give the banker a positive view of you and your business sense. If he finds you prudent in your approach, he will have less to worry about.
- Begin your negotiations with a discussion about interest first, and then talk terms. This is important since your efforts to negotiate good terms can be easily offset by a banker holding the line on interest. Of course, if terms are more important to you, then start with this. Always nail down what is most important first, and then concede on the lesser points.
- Many bankers will not directly offer to help you to qualify for the loan. Though they have the information, and they are often willing to advise you and assist in several ways, they will not volunteer their assistance. You must ask.
- If you find yourself frustrated with hypothetical scenarios, try something like this, *"Okay you've told me all the ways this will not*

work. You are the expert. How can we make it work" or *"If you were in my shoes, what would you do?"*

- If you know you are close, but a junior bank official has denied your loan, you may do some intimidating of your own by going over his or her head. Just threatening to appeal may be sufficient. Nobody likes customers to take problems to their boss.

- Do not be afraid to tell your banker your most intimate (business) secrets. He will probably have forgotten by the time you leave his office, but he will remember that you took him into your confidence about what is really happening in your business.

APPLYING FOR A LOAN AND GETTING A GOOD INTEREST RATE

The Federal Reserve Bank in Australia sets the basis for the calculation of interest rates on all borrowings. It initiates the process by announcing the new bank rate that it proposes to charge the commercial banks. The commercial banks then announce the new overdraft rate it will charge its customers.

Remember that when you ask the bank for a loan you will not be charged the same rate that the bank offers major customers who frequently borrow money. When you see advertisements by banks quoting rates for services, this is the rate for customers like BHP, WOOLWORTHS, and SHELL OIL, not the rate for the average small business owner.

A small business is charged about 3 to 6 percentage points above this rate depending on its credit worthiness and, *in the opinion of the bank,* the ability of the small business to repay borrowings.

WHAT FACTORS DOES A BANK MANAGER TAKE INTO ACCOUNT WHEN APPROVING A LOAN?

Let us look at the situation from the other side of the desk. This will help you in your request for a loan and your negotiations with the bank manager.

Any bank manager will begin from a defensive position, wanting to protect the lenders from shonky deals that could suck the bank's lifeblood. He carries an onerous responsibility and for this reason it is up to you to give a good impression. You should be organized, hardworking and your paperwork must be correct. The degree you will be hassled and grilled depends largely on how you present yourself as a disciplined and committed operator of a viable small business.

Bankers and all people who lend money to businesses consider at least the following factors:

- Convincing evidence that the loan will be repaid.
- Convincing evidence that indicates that you can manage your affairs well enough to ensure the paying back of the loan.
- Convincing evidence that you are sufficiently committed to the business for the bank to feel sure that you will work hard to protect it and make it grow.
- In the worst scenario, if your business fails, the banker needs to feel certain that the value of the business is such that on a disposal of the business, the bank will get their money back.

HOW DO YOU DEAL WITH YOUR BANKER TO ACQUIRE YOUR LOAN?

Whether you are having your annual review of your banking facilities, wish to apply for a loan to refit your premises as required under your lease, or invest in more stock, the following points should be kept in mind when dealing with your banker, so as to achieve the desired result at the lowest possible cost:

- Bankers are impressed only by your standards of management excellence.
- Experience counts heavily in planning, organising, supervising, directing, developing, and demonstrating success in your business.

Arrange your borrowing needs well in advance and keep time on your side. You may be able to shop around. Banks are in competition with each other and you may find an alternate bank willing to negotiate terms such as security margins, interest rates and collateral requirements.

Risk taking must be a calculated decision and the endeavour should not be

a speculative gamble. Remember that bankers are risk avoiders and not risk takers!

Give the bank manager all the information he requires for head office approval of a loan. Although the preparation for a visit to the bank may seem like an enormous amount of work, you will find that being well prepared pays excellent dividends.

Ensure that the loan is big enough to do the job and you will not have to come back for more.

You should provide him with the following evidence that you will be able to repay the loan through the normal running of your business:

- A business plan.
- Cash flow projections for the first 12 months including repayment plans.
- A profit and loss for the first and second year.
- List of assets if any are offered as collateral for the loan.
- A short history of your business experience.
- Your debt paying record in the past.

You need to also take the following into consideration:

Try to negotiate your financial credit needs at your year-end while your financial statements are still correct. Annually arrange a line of credit to meet peak requirements and borrow only what is necessary, when necessary.

- Adjust the loan level as your actual requirements change..
- Make realistic repayment commitments.
- Borrow loans from banks only for specific projects since interest rates on such loans are often cheaper than bank overdrafts.

The bank will usually accept the following as collateral:

- A floating charge or debenture over the entire business.
- Personal guarantees of the proprietor or all partners.
- Outside guarantors like the retailer's main supplier acting as a guarantor.
- The pledging of cash surrender value of life policies.

- The agreement to restrict salaries, drawings and loan repayment of proprietors, partners, or shareholders.
- A mortgage on property if available.
- Collateral over intangible assets that do not appear on the balance sheet.

As one of your conditions for the loan, suggest that your bank manager visit your business. Pick him up if necessary. It is a good idea to take your manager out for a friendly lunch at least every 12 months, to keep the bank informed of how you are doing and what's new in your industry or profession. Good relationships between banker and client are essential and worth the expense and effort.

Remember this is your last option where you have nothing else to lose. If this does not work, then its time to move to a new bank

IN SUMMARY:

- Bankers are almost by nature cautious and conservative.
- Any misleading information, once determined, will destroy the all-important mutual trust required.
- Experience clearly shows that business owners who keep their bankers informed of their successes and lack of it, get the best co-operation when having difficulties.
- Your banker should expect your business to have financial peaks and valleys. So, should you!
- Banking is basically "you give me what I need, and I will give you what you need". But be sure of what you need and what you are prepared to pay for it.
- Try to plan your financing so that your proposal does not appear "desperate".
- Planning is a management quality. It is also a significant criterion for loan proposals. "Urgent" proposals show a weakness in management.
- Never surprise your banker with sudden or unplanned requests for funds.
- Applying for commercial credit can be tedious. It calls for more documentation than you might have initially expected. Don't be disheartened by the amount of paperwork needed to accompany the application. Instead, be prepared.

CHAPTER 16

STOCK SHRINKAGE AND HOW TO STOP IT HAPPENING IN YOUR STORE

In present times, as people run out of money, it is inevitable that some shoplifting will occur. This in turn could result in major stock shrinkage in your store.

Remember you are in business for two reasons. Firstly, to give a service to the public and secondly, to sell your goods at a profit.

You are not in business for theft by your own staff or the shopping public. Neither are you prepared to be the victim of fraudulent or dishonest practices.

The open market concept of retailing, where goods are attractively displayed and customers are invited to personally select what catches their eye, leaves most retailers open prey to professional or amateur shoplifters. A recent report by Checkpoint Security, annual Global Theft Barometer, shows that Australia loses at least $2 billion a year in stock shrinkage. This amounts to 1.4% of total retail sales and it likely to rise further during the present economic decline.

WHERE DOES STOCK SHRINKAGE OCCUR IN YOUR BUSINESS?

According to Checkpoint Security, shrinkage occurs most frequently in the following areas of your business:

Through your employees	40.6%
As a result of shoplifting	36.8%
From internal errors	17.3%
Through suppliers and vendors	5.3%
	100.0%.

Putting shoplifting aside, internal theft remains Australian retailers' biggest loss?

Other studies point out four major differences between retailers with low and high pilferage rates:

1. Retailers with low pilferage are tougher when they apprehend persons caught stealing.
2. They are more likely to prosecute all shoplifters.
3. Low - shrinkage retailers are more conscientious in keeping records of supplier shortages in deliveries.
4. Retailers who minimise shortages set up systems to prevent employee theft.

Australian retailers are starting to install more sophisticated overnight CCTV systems in their stores. Loss prevention methods also include EAS, RFID and analytics, and the use of video verification products. Internet protocol cameras are being used more frequently now making it easier for police to identify and prosecute offenders.

ADT Security has identified "sweet hearting" as a major factor in lost retail revenue. According to its research, 43% of small businesses admit that they or their colleagues provide discounts or freebies to friends and family. The survey showed that the younger the employee the more likely they were to engage in this practice.

According to the Global Barometer, the highest average rates of shrinkage were found to be:

Auto parts, hardware and building materials	1.81%
Apparel clothing and fashion accessories	1.72%
Cosmetics perfume health and beauty and pharmacy	1.70%

The lowest rates of shrinkage were found to be:

Wine, beer, and liquor stores	0.72%
Footwear, shoes and sports goods	0.76%
Electrical, computer centres and electronic stores	0.87%

MEASURING THE TRUE EXTENT OF LOSS DUE TO SHRINKAGE

Things are not always the way they seem – analyse your stock shrinkage carefully.

Having taken stock and ascertained that the gross profit achieved is not what you expected, you could very easily conclude that you have been the victim of stock shrinkage. The best approach is to stop thinking of shortages in terms of gross sales.

If you talk of a shortage of 1.5% of sales, it does not sound too bad or serious but in reality, shrinkage has nothing to do with gross sales. It is in fact a *"direct and actual reduction from net profit"*.

A one-dollar article stolen is a one-dollar loss from the bottom line net profit.

TAKE A CLOSER LOOK

To determine the "real" loss you must calculate how many articles you will have to sell in order to:

1. Recover the cost of the article stolen.
2. Recover the profit that would have been made if the article had not been stolen but sold.

The following example shows how the real loss is calculated.

Example 1

In a store, a baby's dummy is stolen.

Dummy cost	$1 - 50
Sold for	$2 - 00
Profit	$0 - 50

Question:

How many baby's dummies must the retailer sell to recover the cost of the stolen dummy and the profit that would have been made on it if it had not been stolen?

Answer: The retailer must sell 4 baby dummies.

However, the time and wages involved in selling the extra 4 dummies can never be recovered - "they are a dead loss".

REASONS FOR SHRINKAGE

Experience in the retail industry has shown there are many reasons for stock losses. The following is a checklist of major errors resulting in inventory shortage:

A. ERRORS BY SALES ASSISTANTS

- The wrong retail price on a customer's invoice or cash register docket.
- Ringing up the wrong price on the cash register.
- Failure to record regular markdowns on the correct forms.
- Failure to take markdowns on exchanged merchandise returned from customers as defective, as a loss.
- Failure to take markdowns on window damaged goods as a loss.
- Errors in additions on sales dockets.
- Lost "chargeable account" sales dockets.
- Guessing at the price of merchandise that has no price ticket.
- On measured items, a sales assistant may give the customer extra merchandise "for good measure".
- Returned merchandise that is not correctly re-marked at the sold price and then returned to stock at the current price, which may be lower.
- Improper recording of lay-bys.

- Returns to suppliers without getting the appropriate credit note.
- Sales recorded on wrong PLU.
- Sales of multiples (eg 2 for $3.50) processed as 1 for $3.50.
- Computer cost files corrupted by "averaging" and by human intervention.
- Regrouping of several items under a common PLU.
- Incorrect input of cost and selling prices on the point of sale register.
- Incorrect use of "no sale" controls on the register.

B. ERRORS IN HANDLING MERCHANDISE

- Pricing merchandise differently to the amount shown on the invoice. This happens when advertised merchandise at reduced prices is received during a sale.
- Incoming merchandise is not counted accurately or there is a failure to keep records of goods returned.
- With staff collusion and access to scrap bins, merchandise can easily be placed in boxes and then removed from the store.
- Using stock for internal purposes without charging it to an expense account.
- Approving both the original and duplicate invoice for payment.
- If a retailer owns more than one store, goods can be lost in transit between stores.
- Failure to send claim forms to the accounting office for short deliveries,
- Supplier's representatives may pick up merchandise for replacement but fail to replace them.
- Old price tags incorrectly placed onto new stock items.
- Theft from the "back door" after stock has been delivered and recorded but before it is transferred to the stock room or display area.

C. ALERT STAFF CAN HELP TO STOP SHOPLIFTERS

Sales staff are the key to prevent shoplifting.

- Staff should be trained to be assertive, confident, and aware.
- They should serve all customers as quickly as possible.

- Even when the store is busy, customers should be acknowledged as soon as they come into the store. This alerts potential shoplifters that you know they are there.
- Sales staff should check back regularly with customers who wish to browse. Legitimate customers will appreciate the opportunity to ask questions, while shoplifters will feel watched and may leave.
- The salesperson should never turn their back on a customer or leave the sales area unattended. They should develop a warning or alert system to communicate the presence of a suspected shoplifter.
- Employees should be trained to handle cash so they cannot be talked into giving change for a larger bill than was offered, giving change twice, or exchange money with a con artist.
- Arrange an alert system with other traders in your area so that everyone knows when a suspected shoplifter is working your area.

During difficult times reducing stock shrinkage is vital

CHAPTER 17

EFFICIENT PRODUCT BUYING AND HOW TO MAXIMISE YOUR PROFIT FROM EACH SQUARE METRE OF SPACE IN YOUR STORE

As the buyer in your retail business, you must buy in the most efficient manner, ensuring that you maximize the store's profit from each square metre available in your store.

Let us now look at how you can improve the efficiency rating of each line and each department.

INDIVIDUAL LINES

To ensure the best profit per line within your store the most important factors to consider are *the initial mark-ups on merchandise and gross profit after markdowns.*

As the buyer of product for your business, you are constantly being called upon to assess the efficiency rating of the following:

- Selected promotional lines
- High volume sell lines
- High stock lines

A TOUGH MARKET

Today's market is highly competitive. You must market your product against similar products sold by the supermarkets, discount department stores or big specialist stores. Often the only way to compete is with home brand or exclusive products.

It is often hard to decide which line will sell best. Rather than using gut instinct to make that decision, apply the reliable and tested strategy of efficiency ratios.

AN EFFICIENCY RATIO

The formula for this ratio is as follows:

STOCK TURN RATE X 2 PLUS REQUIRED GROSS PROFIT

Example:

In this example we are looking at the efficiency of 3 different lines

	LINE A	LINE B	LINE C
STOCK TURN RATE	3	4	6
MULTIPLED BY 2	6	8	12
PLANNED GROSS PROFIT	40	38	34
EFFICIENCY RATE	46	46	46

Stock turns are multiplied by 2 since most fashion retailers will have at least two seasons per year. If you are not a fashion retailer then ignore step 2 and do not multiply by 2.

A line with a high stock turn rate, but a lower gross profit, can be equal to an item with a low stock turn rate but high gross profit. So, in deciding which line to buy, always select the one with the highest efficiency rating or the one that gives you the most money in the bank. The line with the highest gross profit is often not the one that provides the most money in the bank.

This technique can be used for the rating of each department in your store as well and it should be carried out at least every quarter.

To keep ahead of your competition, a department which consistently rates low on the efficiency rating system should be closed.

HOW TO MAXIMISE YOUR PROFIT FROM EACH SQUARE METRE OF SPACE IN YOUR STORE

Example

Although retail sales or profits may rise or fall, there is one constant in your business and that is *the size of your store*. The cost of renting this area is expensive. To simplify calculations, we will express the total occupancy costs of the retailer at, $400 per square metre when comparing it with other retailers.

When comparing similar businesses of differing sizes, we can then express sales at $8,500 per square metre. In this way we can bring the comparison to a common form of measurement. It is then easily understood by others.

An especially useful management technique is to measure the performance of the business as it relates to the sales and the gross profit earned by each department every month, according to the area that we have allocated to that department.

The following example is of a typical pharmacy by department. It clearly shows the performance of each department.

TYPICAL PHARMACY: ANALYSIS OF SALES BY TRADING AREA YEAR ENDING JUNE 2022

Front of Shop Analysis

DEPARTMENT	SIZE Sq. Mtr	SALES FOR YEAR	GROSS PROFIT YEAR	SALES AS % OF FRONT OF SHOP	GROSS PROFIT AS % FRONT OF SHOP	SIZE AS % FRONT OF SHOP	SALES RATING BY VALUE	GP RATING BY VALUE	RATING DEPT BY SIZE
Coughs & Colds	5.25	104,732	42,945	14.68	16.57	4.35	1	1	9
Skin Care	6.60	97,554	33,168	13.68	12.80	5.47	2	2	7
Syringes	1.00	64,000	27,600	8.97	10.65	0.83	3	3	24
General Medicine	1.60	62,647	23,926	8.78	9.23	1.33	4	4	20
Analgesics	3.00	53,167	18,545	7.45	7.16	2.49	5	5	13

Hair Care	6.00	36,036	12,621	5.05	4.87	4/98	6	7	8
Baby	12.00	35,774	14,310	5.02	5.52	9.95	7	6	1
Vitamins	4.50	35,646	10,393	4.86	4.01	3.73	8	8	10
Eye & Ear	1.30	24,482	8,079	3.43	3.12	1.08	9	9	23
Fragrance	9.00	21,134	7,396	2.96	2.85	7.46	10	10	4
Stomach & Gut	3.00	20,943	6,701	2.94	2.59	2.49	11	11	14
Wound Care	4.50	16,282	4,884	2.28	1.88	3.73	12	15	12
Mens	7.50	15,696	5,965	2.20	2.30	6.22	13	12	6
Sports Medicine	4.50	13,988	5,315	1.96	2.05	3.73	14	14	11
Other	10.50	12,686	5,708	1.78	2.20	8.71	15	13	3
Womens Cosmetics	9.00	12,007	3,602	1.68	1.39	7.46	16	18	5
Photographics	0.75	9,863	2,465	1.38	0.95	0.62	17	20	27
Misc/Cash Desks	11.75	9,120	3,648	1.28	1.41	9.74	18	17	2
Oral Hygiene	1.80	8,384	1,677	1.18	0.65	1.49	19	24	18
Confectionary	1.00	7,968	3,984	1.12	1.54	0.83	20	16	25
Family Planning	0.50	7,685	1,537	1.08	0.59	0.41	21	26	30
Foot Care	0.75	7,115	2,277	1.00	0.88	0.62	22	21	28
Asthma	2.25	6,527	2,611	0.92	1.01	1.87	23	19	17
Sun Care	1.50	6,079	2,128	0.85	0.82	1.24	24	22	21
Antacids	3.00	5,605	1,905	0.79	0.74	2.49	25	23	15
Household	0.75	5,512	1,543	0.77	0.60	0.62	26	25	29
Hand & Nails	1.50	5,430	1,358	0.76	0.52	1.24	27	27	22
Home Health Care	3.00	3,520	1,056	0.49	0.41	2.49	28	29	16
Diabetes	1.80	3,030	1,212	0.42	0.47	1.49	29	28	19
Feminine Hygiene	1.00	1,692	609	0.24	0.23	0.83	30	30	26
TOTAL FRONT OF SHOP	120.60	713,305	259,168	100.00	100.	100.00			
DISPENS – GOVT	25.40	1,570,000	669,824						
DISPENS – PATIENT		523,695							
TOTAL PHARMACY	146.00	2,807,000	928,992						

ANALYSIS OF PHARMACY LAYOUT SALES AND PROFITABILITY

- The department with the largest area, namely baby products, produces the 7th highest sales and the 6th highest gross profit.
- The cash desks which are meant for impulse and miscellaneous

products such as lollies usually carry high mark-ups, and are obviously not working for the pharmacy as they rank only 17th in gross profit.
- Two of the smallest departments, namely syringes and general medicine, are the 3rd and 4th best in both sales and gross profit.
- Two high profile departments, namely diabetes and feminine hygiene, perform worst in the pharmacy.

Clearly the pharmacy has not been laid out in a way that maximises sales and profitability.

More space needs to be allocated to successful departments in the front of the shop and less space allocated to less profitable departments. Unfortunately, though not profitable, some departments may have to be maintained due to customer needs and demands.

CHAPTER 18

IS YOUR SUPPLIER GIVING YOU A GOOD DEAL?

You may buy product from a supplier who generally services you and other similar retailers in your category. But, is he a good supplier and do his products help you to achieve the overall gross margin you are aiming for in your business?

Often you find when dealing with a supplier, in order for you to achieve at least a further 10% reduction in cost, you may have to buy 6 of a product. If you do so and at the end of the season you are left with say 2 of those items, then you must get rid of those products at well below cost. Therefore, you are driving down your gross margin.

HOW TO MEASURE THE PERFORMANCE OF YOUR SUPPLIER?

One of the best techniques for monitoring the performance of a supplier is to include a two-digit supplier code in each stock item's code number. Thus, from your stock control system, when producing a quarterly or 6 monthly, or even a seasonal trading account, you will be able to prepare a trading account by major supplier.

Example:

If the strategy of your business is to mark up the cost of each product by 100%, you will be making a first gross profit of 50%.

You will also know from experience with sales, markdowns, and shrinkage, that this gross profit is reduced to 42%. It is also the basis you used to set your budget for the year or season.

It follows, that if you take out a trading account for a supplier whose product you can track through the stock system by his code number, it will show the following result for the season:

Suppler A	
Sales of Shoes for season	$50000
Less Cost of sales	32000
Gross profit	18000
% Gross profit to sales	36%
Budget % Gross profit to sales	42%

As you can see from this example, this supplier will not be profitable for your business.

Suggestion:

The next time you meet with this supplier do not be afraid of discussing the following:

- Show him the seasonal account of his supply to you.
- Point out to him how using your open to buy programme, you were forced to discount the last unsold items of his product at the end of the season in order to clear stock, and that this has had a major negative impact on your gross margin.
- Suggest to him that you can only continue using him as a supplier if he gives you an extra 10% on 3 products (not 6). In this way you will be avoiding the loss of extra margin at the end of the season.
- Or even suggest that it is time to negotiate a new price structure if he wishes to remain a supplier with your retail business.

Know your suppliers and you will be surprised at what better buying deals you can achieve.

CHAPTER 19

GROWING YOUR BUSINESS SUCCESSFULLY

The balance sheet of a company is often compared to a sponge. The sponge absorbs water while the balance sheet soaks up cash. As the sponge nears its capacity to absorb additional water it becomes increasingly less efficient. The same occurs with your business.

Increasing sales or growth creates a need for additional money to finance an increased level of assets. Although the business may attract an injection of funds by the owner, injecting capital, or by taking in a partner, the main source of finance is from debt. This is risky. Any increase in interest expenses could put pressure on profits.

Growth in sales is often accompanied by a decrease in efficiency of operation. Proportionately, more assets are required to support new sales so that the rate of assets growth increases faster than sales - you make the same percent of profit, but you make it less efficiently.

SMARTER AND BETTER

If you want to survive this economic downturn and expand your business successfully, you must manage growth better. One method of achieving this is by adopting the following management techniques:

- Manage your current assets, particularly stock and stock-turns, more efficiently.

- Restructure your debt between long-term and short-term debt.
- Sell your unproductive assets.
- Close your inefficient departments within the business.
- Control your expansion program. Each growth step is evaluated before proceeding with the next one.
- Lease instead of buying your assets.
- Implement sale and leaseback of your existing assets.
- Accept the concept of more risk.
- Bring in a partner.

BE PROACTIVE

It is a human failing that we often wait until we are sick before we go to the doctor, or in Australian terms, "if it ain't broke don't fix it". We normally wait for the symptoms to appear and then respond to problems. But this can be too late.

We love to call this the Australian entrepreneurial spirit, the 'gut feel' approach or 'going for broke.' There is nothing wrong with this attitude, but we need to put it into a structure and framework that capitalises on our business strengths and shores up our business weaknesses.

SKIN DEEP

Problems in your business are solved when you examine the deeper causes. As in medicine, treating the symptoms of a disease alone will not cure it.

Business owners often erroneously blame the poor health of their business on low cash, low gross margin, and low net profit. What an excuse for poor business management and performance!

If you study the information provided and apply it in time you will turn your present difficulties around and emerge as a more organised and financially viable small business. More importantly, your resilience will enable you to survive the peaks and troughs of an ever-changing financial climate for small businesses in Australia.

A RETAILER OPEN TO BUY PROGRAMME ------ BASED ON CURRENT STOCKS AND SALES SEPTEMBER 2020 TO FEBRUARY 2021

OPEN TO BUY TARGET	SEP	OCT	NOV	DEC	JAN	FEB
OPENING STOCK	1000	2100	2800	2500	1400	1200
ON ORDER	2400	1800	850	600	500	450
SUB – TOTAL	3400	3900	3650	3100	1900	1650
COST OF SALES	1300	1100	1150	1700	700	550
PROJECTED CLOSING STOCK	2250	2850	2400	1250	1350	1550
BUDGETTED CLOSING STOCK	2100	2800	2500	1400	1200	1000
OPEN TO BUY	150	50	-100	-150	150	550
O.T.B. YEAR TO DATE	150	200	100	-50	100	650

ASSUMPTIONS:
1. OPENING STOCK=1000 CLOSING STOCK = $1000
2. STOCK TURN 6 TIMES P.A
3. CLOSING STOCK AT MONTH END MUST BE NEXT 2 MONTHS SALES
4. CANNOT BUY ANY EXESS STOCK
5. ASSUME COST OF SALES FOR MARCH IS $800 AND APRIL IS $750

PART 2

LEASE
NEGOTIATION

THE COVID-19 CRISIS AND ITS AFFECT ON RETAIL BUSINESSES AND LANDLORDS OF RETAIL PREMISES

The Covid.19 crises has had a major impact on retail businesses worldwide. Australia has been no exception.

Due to Lockdowns in many states and territories, turnover of retail business has fallen by up to 80%. This has placed stress on many retailers and resulted in their inability to meet their monthly rent payments and meet other obligations under their leases.

Landlords are also suffering because of falling rent income and the cancellation of tenancies. Victorian properties, especially, have experienced the worst impact with property values falling substantially, some estimate falls between 10% and 20%, and even more.

As some retailers are involved in state appeal tribunals concerning their rent, many disputes are being settled outside the appeal system but some retailers are paying no rental while their stores in shopping centres are closed. In this situation, retail rentals are likely to continue to decline and property values may fall.

In March 2020, the Federal Government introduced a national plan to protect tenants that included an eviction moratorium under which evictions are not allowed.

For instance, in Victoria, which has been the hardest hit for retailers, an act was introduced entitled the Commercial Tenancy Relief Scheme. The scheme provided for the following support:

- A six-month moratorium on commercial tenancy evictions for the non-payment of rent in small to medium enterprises with an annual turnover under $50 million, and that have experienced a minimum 30% reduction in turnover due to Covid-19 commencing from 29 March 2020. This moratorium was extended for a further six months, but has now ended.
- A freeze on rent increases during the moratorium.
- A rental payment waiver or deferral taking into account, the tenants

PART 2
LEASE NEGOTIATION

income reduction due to Covid-19 to be negotiated between tenant and landlord.

- A free mediation service for commercial tenants and landlords as assessed through the Victorian State Business Council to support fair tenancy negotiations.

The pandemic has also accelerated ecommerce penetration into Australian Retail. More and more consumers are now buying online, a practice which may become permanent in the future. This will mean that retailers may require less retail space for their stores than they currently enjoy and pay rental.

PART 2
LEASE NEGOTIATION

CHAPTER 20

LEASE NEGOTIATION

WHAT ARE THE 8 GOLDEN RULES OF NEGOTIATING A RETAIL LEASE?

Negotiating a retail lease is not the result of mere luck but comes from sound and active management.

1. Do your homework and know what rentals are being paid in your area by other retailers.
2. Scrutinise all clauses of your lease. Ask relevant questions and make certain that you finalise all aspects of your lease during negotiation so that the final lease reflects the agreement of all parties involved and has no surprises.
3. In resolving lease issues, the best approach is to think like a landlord and not a retailer. This may not be easy but will provide you with an excellent outcome.
4. Always think ahead and consider what the impact of deregulation on your retail store will be, for example pharmacists or other professional organisations.
5. "Fitting out" costs is expensive so ask the landlord to make a fit-out contribution to this cost.
6. Consider all the hidden costs involved. These include, legal fees, stamp duty, consulting fees, design fees, plan approval fees, survey fees, lease registration, lease preparation fees as well as any sundry costs.

7. If you are taking over a lease on the purchase of a retail store, always ask a consultant to make a due diligence check of the lease to ensure that you have at least five years of the lease outstanding.

8. if you have an interest in several retail stores, ensure that you have a corporate structure in place, so that if one store fails your other stores are not affected.

PART 2
LEASE NEGOTIATION

CHAPTER 21

WHAT IS A RETAIL LEASE?

A retail lease is a document for a pre-negotiated period allowing a retailer, in exchange for the payment of rental, to occupy premises owned by a landlord. If at the end of the period, the landlord decides that he does not wish to renew the lease there is nothing to stop him letting the premises to someone else. This is an important point to remember as many people enter into lease agreements with the expectation that they will be offered a lease renewal.

PARTIES AUTOMATICALLY PART OF A LEASE

There are several participants involved in any lease negotiation for a retail tenancy. It is important to realize that what each participant seeks to gain from the negotiations is different, and will quite often be in conflict.

The participants to any retail lease negotiations are the following:

A. THE LANDLORD/LESSOR

Generally, the landlord seeks to secure the following from the lease negotiations:

- An optimum rental for the available space with minimum expenditure. He expects the retailer to be responsible for paying as much of the maintenance and the costs of upkeep as possible.
- The landlord seeks a retailer who has the resources to pay the rent and outgoings over the term of the lease.
- The landlord will seek a watertight lease ensuring that his rights are

fully protected. As the landlord is responsible for preparing the lease it is often initially written by the landlord in his favour. The advent of Covid-19 has changed the wording of such leases considerably.

Landlords generally fall into 3 categories:

- Landlords of retail shopping centres, complexes or malls.
- Landlords of single shops, who are often private investors with properties in strips or stand-alone premises.
- Landlords who own commercial properties that may have shops located in a specific area such as shops on the ground floor of buildings.

If the premises are in Victoria, this may include landlords who have tenants on the first three levels of a commercial building who sell goods and services, and who may be covered by the Victorian Retail Tenancy Legislation. Some of the tenants maybe accounting or legal firms.

The Australian Capital Territory is the only state where there is a commercial business zoning for retail tenancy legislation. The zoning covers retail premises with an area of less than 300m2 that are not involved in the sale or hire of goods that fall under the retail tenancy legislation. This zoning usually does not apply to shopping centres.

B. THE RETAILER/LESSEE

Lease negotiations usually allow a retailer or business proprietor to assess whether specific conditions will permit the profitable operation of a business and the development of the goodwill value of that business. As a result, the retailer will be seeking the following key aspects from the lease:

- The ability to conduct a profitable business.
- An affordable rent for the duration of the lease.
- Security of tenure for the desired time.
- Protection from competition, particularly if the retail premises are in a shopping centre or even a strip centre where several shops are owned by the same landlord.
- Conditions in the lease that will ensure non-interference in the day to day running of the business.

- Conditions that will not impose additional financial burdens on the business.
- The ability to sell the business and assign the lease with as few problems as possible so as to maximize the goodwill built up in the business.

A letting agent is often the first port of call for many retailers seeking retail premises in a non-shopping centre environment. However, several of the larger real estate agents also manage and lease space in small shopping centres. The agent often handles all the initial documentation during the negotiation process and usually receives a fee from the landlord for entering the lease. The agent usually has an administration agreement with the landlord and carries out various duties as agreed upon with the landlord.

Some of the recent changes to retail tenancy legislation, particularly in Victoria now impose on the agent, the same responsibilities, and liabilities as the landlord

D. THE SOLICITOR

There are usually two solicitors that act for parties to a lease. One is employed by the landlord and will prepare the lease from the commercial lease offer negotiated by the landlord's leasing executive or the landlord's agent. The other, is the solicitor for the retailer who advises on the retailer's legal position. In addition, many retailers engage the services of a leasing consultant to help negotiate the lease and prepare a commercial report on the lease document written by the landlord's solicitor. Frequently, the consultant's report is combined with the one presented by the retailer's solicitor.

In the case of franchisees, the retailer's solicitor will often prepare the franchise agreement at the same time so that its duration may coincide with the term of the lease.

E. ASSIGNORS AND ASSIGNEES

If a retailer wishes to sell the business during the term of the lease, he or she becomes known as the assignor. This means that he or she will require the approval from the landlord for the assignment of the remainder of the lease to the purchaser of the business.

THE LAW RELATING TO RETAIL TENANCIES IN AUSTRALIA

The Australian Constitution provides the states and territories with the power to enact retail tenancy legislation. In Australia, the laws relating to retail tenancies can differ between jurisdictions.

It is important for retailers to be aware that if they were to open a retail store in another state, they may find that a number of clauses dealing with rent, outgoings, market reviews, tenancy mix and a number of others clauses may vary from state to state, even when the landlord may be the same.

TYPES OF LEASES ENTERED INTO BY RETAILERS

A retailer in a shopping centre needs to appreciate that a shopping centre has a broad tenancy mix and that landlords can enter into different leases. Your lease depends on the type of tenant you are - a specialty store, a pharmacy, a coffee shop, a supermarket, or a mini major department store.

Some leases will have the protection of the Retail Tenancy Legislation and others will not. The key to this protection by the Act is that if a clause in the lease is contrary to the provisions of that Act then the wording of that clause is void. If there is a dispute the provisions of the Act will apply.

There are several basic lease conditions that the parties to a lease cannot negotiate or contract out of. These include the minimum lease term, charging of legal expenses, conditions dealing with relocation or demolition of the premises, methods of calculating market rents, and methods of calculating outgoings and restrictions on assignment. The State Acts specifically covers all these provisions.

In the case of a departmental store or supermarket, the leases will usually be based on a nominal base rent per month or/plus a percentage on sales, whichever is the higher. These leases usually provide for rates and taxes to be paid together with certain specified outgoings attributable to that tenancy. Particularly, large outgoing costs like management fees, centre management costs and security costs are often excluded.

For stores of a size of around 400 square meters plus, (known as mini majors) the lease will usually be based on a low rent per square metre plus a full share of outgoings, or even a gross rent comprising the two.

For speciality stores, the lease will usually be calculated on a much higher rent per sq. metre, as well as a full share of outgoings. Jewellery shops and fashion operators tend to pay the highest rental per square meter in a shopping centre, as do food outlets despite the food outlets occupying only a small area.

Stores in strip centres usually have only a base rent component plus statutory municipal charges and land tax. Sometimes, insurance is also payable. Land tax is specifically legislated not to be paid by the retailer in some states.

Figures from URBIS, (which are often quoted by landlords in negotiations as the benchmark for your retail category) sometimes, group retail categories such as pharmacies are grouped with cosmetics. Any pharmacist will know that these are two different market sectors and have no relationship. It is well documented that cosmetic stores have a smaller retail footprint and others have "island locations" in the middle of the mall. These formats have higher rentals. Thus, combining this format with pharmacy data, increases the average rental per square metre giving misleading information regarding "expected rents". Other retailers in similar situations need to watch out for similar groupings.

IN WHAT NAME IS THE LEASE TO BE ENTERED INTO?

It is important to carefully consider the entity that will enter the lease on behalf of the retailer. For example, a private company, public company, trust, partnership, or a store in the name of an individual or partnership.

In the case of a private company, the directors of that company may have to guarantee the lease. In the event of an individual or partnership, everyone automatically guarantees the lease with all their private assets. These assets could become available to be taken by the lessor in the event of a default of the lease.

If you are for example, a pharmacist, naturopath, psychologist or optometrist forming part of a medical clinic, (that is in a shopping centre or in a stand-alone clinic) you may only be a sub-lessee of one of the doctors who holds the head lease. It is therefore imperative that your sub-lease is structured in a way that it allows you or the other medical professionals to move in and out of the clinic without disturbing the lease. It may be prudent to secure the lease in the name of a management company or service company for the clinic with each participant holding a share in the management or service-company.

The most asked question by retailers before in entering into a lease is "how much is the rent?" The answer is not that simple, as landlords may require several components that make up the final total rent payable. So, always read the small print of your lease and disclosure statement very carefully.

PART 2
LEASE NEGOTIATION

CHAPTER 22

RENT

WHAT IS RENT?

The courts have defined rent as "a sum of money that a person has contracted to pay for the use of property for a term". The way a retailer structures the payment of rent can often determine how profitable the business may be.

The best rent package that can be negotiated by a retailer is a gross rent deal (This includes a total occupancy figure covering rent, statutory and variable outgoings). If rent is payable in a shopping centre it includes the marketing levy as well. It is important for the retailer to know exactly what the total rental will be without any additional charges.

The next best rent package to consider, is one in which a retailer pays a negotiated net rent amount and where the outgoings for the current year are the "base_amount_". It is worth noting that outgoings during the lease period are only payable on the proportion of the amount more than the base amount when the lease was entered.

Most speciality leases are calculated on an agreed cost per sq. metre plus outgoings based on the proportion that the area of the retailers shop bears to the gross lettable area of the centre or complex.

Since Covid-19 several rentals have been calculated on a percentage of sales for the previous month. The advantage, of this to the retailer is that rent is payable monthly in arrear with a possible saving in cash flow, at least for the first month

RENT FREE PERIODS

As an inducement to a retailer to enter a lease, a landlord may offer a rent-free period in the first year. This will provide the retailer with an initial cash saving to be set off against the high cost of fitting out and stocking the store.

Such incentives have become quite common particularly when existing shopping centres are being refurbished and the landlord is trying to attract new types of tenants to the centre.

Rent free periods are also frequently offered where a store has remained unoccupied for some time and the landlord is keen to attract a good retailer. This has been especially relevant during the Covid-19 period.

Therefore, a retailer should always try to negotiate an initial rent-free period of about 3 to 6 months. This will allow trading properly before rent is payable. The downside is that the retailer will have to contribute to outgoings from day one.

PERCENTAGE RENT PAYABLE

Some shopping centre leases usually include an additional rental known as percentage rental. This rental is usually calculated on an agreed percentage of sales (depending on the industry) less the base rental. It is often regarded by a retailer as an attempt by the landlord to gain additional rental if the business is successful and achieves better than projected sales.

As these percentage rents are structured around a base rental, this effectively means that the landlord is sharing the good times of a retail store without sharing any of the risks. Recently, it has become standard management practice in leases to have percentage rent clauses.

This is an example of how the percentage rental is calculated

Sales for Year are	$500000
Agreed percentage rental	8%
Base rent for Year	$38000

Thus, percentage rent is calculated as follows

$500000 x 8%	$40,000
Less Base Rental for year	$38,000
Percentage Rent Payable	$2000

From a landlord's perspective, receiving some annual percentage rental may be valuable, however this is not the reason for this clause. Landlords under the various retail tenancy acts in Australia are not permitted to ask the tenants to provide the sales figures of the business. By using this technique of a percentage rental clause, they are thus entitled to obtain the retailers sales figures annually and can check if any percentage rental is payable.

Calculating the percentage rent allows the landlord or the agent to determine what rental the tenant can afford in future lease negotiations, and at the same time allows him to plan for the future management and development of the centre.

For example, pharmacy retailers could argue that they cannot pay percentage rent as the Pharmacy Act prevents a retailer from sharing his or her income with someone who is not a retailer, as provided in Section 92© Pharmacy Practice Act 2004 (Victoria).

However, the pharmacy retailer may agree to provide sales figures based on the front of shop sales plus NHS revenue (not the value of the scripts). Many shopping centre landlords are operating on this principle.

ANNUAL RENT REVIEWS

Most leases, provide for a regular annual review of rents with no ceiling on the amount of the increase or decrease. A so called "ratchet clause" (where rents can only go up) have now been abolished in all states.

Under the retail legislation, it is a requirement that a clearly defined formula be set out in the lease document - for example, 5% fixed increase per annum or CPI or a market review. In Victoria, CPI + 2% as a combination is not permitted.

If the formula is not included specifically in the lease, then no variation of rent is possible unless all parties agree.

Given that CPI increases are not common for all states, a retailer in Perth for example, may have a larger CPI base than a retailer in Melbourne. To smooth out fluctuations for a retailer operating in a number of states, it may be useful for him to request that the CPI formula to be used is the average CPI over the eight capital cities and not the CPI of the city where the store is located.

IS THE RENT ASKED REASONABLE?

This is a particularly important question to ask, especially if the terms of the lease include a market review of rent in years four of a five of the lease.

Before agreeing to the final rent and outgoings that a retailer believes is affordable, the retailer should prepare a profit and loss statement over the full period of the lease, showing anticipated sales growths and gross profit projections.

To do this, deduct your anticipated labour costs, advertising, and other store expenses as well as the expected store profit in your budget. This will show a balance that represents the profit you can anticipate earning before occupancy costs. Then, add the occupancy cost showing the impact of possible high, medium, and low market rent review scenarios.

It is important to note, that if a retailer cannot achieve the anticipated profit percentage to sales that he is budgeting for using the high market review scenario during the lease term, the initial base year rent and outgoings' negotiation with the landlord will needs to be reviewed. This is a sure sign that the landlord is asking for a premium for being in that centre that is over and above what you can probably afford.

OPTION RENEWALS AND EXERCISING YOUR OPTION UNDER THE TERMS OF THE LEASE

Your management schedule will alert you to the date by which you need to exercise your option.

Remember that an option in a lease is a right that every retailer has and is not the right of the landlord. The retailer alone can decide whether he will exercise the option or not.

PART 2
LEASE NEGOTIATION

The landlord may be anxious until the retailer formally exercises the option. He will be uncertain whether the retailer will continue in occupation or whether he will have to find a new retailer, even at a reduced rental. Retailers may use this opportunity to improve conditions in their lease by requesting the landlord to vary certain lease conditions. Problem clauses may be altered at this stage, due to the landlord's vulnerability.

However, a retailer's ability to take advantage of the situation is likely to be determined by the way the parties negotiated the original option terms of the lease.

Retailers should not accept a clause that grants an option in the lease that further provides for the cancellation of this option, should the landlord wish to redevelop or refurbish that part of the shopping centre.

Retailers should also avoid types of clauses that provide for "due and punctual performance" of all the terms and conditions of the lease throughout the term as a pre-condition to the exercise of an option. The retailer's solicitor should water down such a clause to ensure that the retailer can exercise such a option if he or she is not in breach of the lease (at the time of the notice exercising the option or at the expiration of the term of the lease).

CHAPTER 23

OUTGOINGS

NEGOTIATING OUTGOINGS PAYABLE BY THE RETAILER

Most leases are calculated on a base rental plus outgoings therefore it is essential that all retailers understand exactly what this entails.

In a shopping centre, all the retail Acts require the landlord to provide the retailer with a schedule of outgoings that forms part of the pool of outgoings. Based on this schedule, the tenant will be required to pay outgoings to the landlord. The payment is usually monthly, based on a rate per square meter for such outgoings.

Some major retailers often do not pay for some outgoings like administration fees which is a large outgoing amount, and small retailers should try to exclude such outgoings if possible.

As the rate for outgoings in some larger shopping centres is now more than $225 per square meter, this is an extremely important component of the total rental package.

ADVICE FOR RETAILERS

If, the landlord quotes you an outgoings rate per square metre, you should ensure that you know precisely which outgoings that rate covers.

Some outgoings schedules include municipal council and water rates and if applicable a land tax charge, while others do not. If these outgoings are excluded from the rate, you will probably be billed either directly by the State Authority or the centre will pay the account and recover it from the retailer periodically throughout the financial year.

When calculating your occupancy cost before signing the lease, make sure that you include all outgoing charges both "direct and indirect".

Remember that in some states like Queensland, South Australia and Victoria, land tax is no longer recoverable as an outgoing from retailers. Therefore, make certain that you are given a current schedule of outgoings with your disclosure statement and ask your solicitor to check that each item on the schedule is covered by a corresponding clause in the lease. This ensures that in later years any new outgoing expenses cannot be included without your permission.

As indicated above, the management and administration charge of the centre is one of the largest outgoings expenses charged by the landlord. Ask the landlord to tell you exactly how this cost is made up. He should tell you the precise amount represented by centre management, salaries, wages and office expenses In addition, he should reveal how the "basis" of the corporate head office was calculated , as well as the "basis" that the corporate head office expenses was allocated between all the shopping centre owned by that landlord.

Note that in West Australia, management fees are not recoverable as an outgoing from retailers and in Victoria, management fees are capped by the increase in CPI for the year.

AIR CONDITIONING

Air Conditioning costs and their apportionment to retailers has become a source of contention between the landlord and the retailer.

Although, one centralised system seems to service the entire centre, landlords contend that the major anchor tenants have their own air-conditioning systems and as a result, their leases do not provide for them having to bear any share of the air-conditioning expenses. Naturally, this has resulted in an imbalance in the area proportion over which such costs are made.

REPAIRS AND MAINTENANCE

Repairs and Maintenance is another large expense in the outgoing schedule. It is advisable to obtain a breakdown of how these costs are calculated into building repairs, electrical, signs, car parks, locks and keys, glass and so on.

In Victoria, the Act has been changed to make landlords more responsible for paying for repairs and maintenance. These costs should not be included in the outgoings schedule payable by the tenant. In addition, any costs in respect of the safety of the building, has also been deemed to be the expense of the landlord and not an outgoing (However this is still under appeal in the courts).

The latest amendment to the Act in Victoria, allows for essential safety measures(ESM) can be recovered by the landlord as an outgoing for maintenance, as well as to an installation which a tenant has agreed to pay relating to the fit out of the premises.

Alert yourself to the possibility of capital expenditure being included in this outgoing cost particularly where a shopping centre is under refurbishment.

If you are in a strip centre that may be subject to flooding from storms, always insist that the lease contains a condition requiring the landlord to ensure that the premises are water and weather sealed on the handover of the premises.

TYPICAL RETAILER'S CHECKLIST OF OUTGOINGS EACH YEAR

A. GROSS LETTABLE AREA

- Is the G.L.A the same as it was in the previous year?
- If not, establish why these are reasons for change.
- Check the G.L.A reconciliation form to establish whether the landlord has changed the basis of calculating the G.L.A.
- Does the G.L.A. as calculated, conform to the definition in the lease and disclosure statement? This is a key point.
- If renovations or refurbishments are taking place in the centre over the 30th June period, check whether any additional area has been

taken into account in determining the GLA calculation in the budget provided by the centre.

- If there are free-standing tenancies at the centre, for example service stations, fast food outlets and so on, check if these have been considered in the GLA calculation.
- Has the office area of the shopping centre been deducted from the GLA? Some landlords have taken legal opinion that has not as yet been challenged, in order to deduct this area from the GLA. Challenge this if you are in doubt.
- Has the number of kiosks in the centre remained the same as last year? If kiosks are removed, then the area of the kiosk should be included in the common area and deducted from the GLA. If new kiosks are erected, the GLA should increase and the common area should be decreased.

B. RETAILERS OWN SIZE OF PREMISES

- Has the size of your premises changed from last year?
- Is the size of your premises still as stated in the lease? If not you should have confirmation on file to this effect. This may include downsizing of premises during the year.
- If the size of your premises is calculated on a percentage of the total centre, always check the reference schedule of your lease to see how many decimal places the calculation is to be computed. This may seem a minor matter, but mistakes are often made to the retailer's detriment.
- The outgoings apportionment, should be on same basis as stated in the reference schedule of the lease.

Be certain that the same percentage is used in apportionment from year to year.

C. VARIABLE OUTGOINGS – A GENERAL CHECK LIST

Take the following steps to ascertain any variances in the outgoings you are charged:

- From the schedule supplied to you by the centre management, prepare a comparison between current year's outgoings and the following budget year, and note any variances.

- On receipt of the actual audited outgoings, prepare a comparison between the actual and the budget for year and note any variances.

- Then prepare a comparison of the actual audited outgoings for the previous year with the budget for the following year and note any variances.

- Compare the above variances with the assumptions made by the centre in the preparation of the budget to ensure that the data is still valid. If you detect a major variance that is not in your favour, request an explanation from centre management. If an unsatisfactory explanation is given, request that they revise the budget, so providing you with an effecting a saving in cash flow during the budget year.

- Check the outgoings that you have been charged with the actual lease provisions. If the charge is not specifically contained in the lease, raise a query with the centre. If the charge is due to interpretation of lease wording, query this as well. In Victoria, the outgoings must benefit the premises in order to be charged to the retailer. Therefore, if your premises are on the outside of a centre you should not have to pay for escalators or air conditioning.

- If you have more than one retail store, compare your analysis of the above points with the landlord's other centres to see if any common trend emerges. This will alert you to the possibility of errors in the charges.

- If there were any concessions obtained or negotiated with the landlord in a previous year, ascertain that they have carried forward to the budget year.

- If your retail store trades outside the normal working hours of the centre for example, until 9pm each night, you should try to negotiate that your specific trading hours stated in the lease are separate from the centres basic trading hours, so that any costs after the centres normal trading hours are not charged to you. This is often applicable to video shops and pharmacists who often trade after normal trading hours.

- If you are trading outside normal trading hours of the centre, and are forced to pay a fee per hour to the centre for this, you need to ensure that you are not paying twice. Check whether this payment for after-hours expenses was deducted from the pool of outgoings before the balance of the pool is allocated to tenants.

D. VARIABLE OUTGOINGS - SPECIFIC EXPENSES IN SHOPPING CENTRES

Tenants in strip centres or in stand- alone locations, often only pay rates, taxes and insurance costs. Tenants in shopping centres are usually charged the undermentioned costs. The Tenancy Acts in most states usually state the amount that can be charged and any unusual costs, or the charge for "sundry costs" should immediately be questioned.

1. Security

- Some landlords include a proviso, after the preamble to the outgoings clause that management's responsibility includes, "operation and management," of the centre. This includes security of the centre.
- As you are paying for security you should insist that your lease or leases include the words "and securing the centre". This may assist your insurance company recovering a theft claim if the centre fails to provide adequate security.

2. Air Conditioning

- Ensure that the cost of air conditioning of cinemas will be borne directly by the cinema operator. Also ensure that the cost of air-conditioning of cinema foyers is not included with the common areas of the centre.
- Be aware that electricity charges for running air conditioning plants can be purchased by the centre at bulk rates and charged to retailers at normal rates. A good way of finding out if this is happening would be to compare your store electricity costs per square metre with the common area cost to see if there is a difference.

3. Cleaning

- Note that the expense of cleaning may include salary costs of the cleaner employed by the centre. Unless the lease provides otherwise, ensure that only the basic salary is charged and not provisions made for long service or annual leave.

- Cleaning may include waste removal. If your lease specifically excludes "wet refuse", ensure that this is deducted.
- Check to see if cleaning costs include cleaning of food courts and salary costs of waitressing for common areas. Most new leases should provide for such costs to be borne by food court retailers directly.
- Often food court expenses are charged to food court operators as a "marketing levy" based on the total cost divided by the number of food court operators. This avoids the provisions of the Tenancy Acts that require the costs to be charged to retailers on the basis that the ratio of the area of the store bears to the area of the centre.
- If the centre includes an office tower, check the apportionment of cost between common areas of each floor of offices and centre common areas. Note, that In New South Wales cleaning has to be split by the landlord between cleaning costs and consumable cleaning expenses.

4. Insurance

- Establish the basis of insurance apportionment for groups of landlords who have a portfolio of properties. Often this basis is established on the value of buildings. If a landlord has a major property and the value has fallen dramatically, other centres including a centre where your store is located, may be absorbing a higher insurance allocation.
- In the case of centres owned by insurance companies, establish how the insurance cost was determined, and whether the cost is an internal "charge" or it represents a true market charge.
- If insurance rates have generally fallen in Australia, enquire why a particular centre has not followed the national trend. Your own insurer is often a good source of information.
- The high cost of public liability insurance, needs to be carefully examined by lease administrators. For instance, major landlords who operate on a worldwide basis have in the past been hard hit by terrorism threats in the USA and Europe. As a result, their world insurance costs have been were particularly hard "hit", including their Australian centres even though Australia may not have the same risks as Europe or the USA.

- Any excess on a claim that is to be borne by the lessor, can sometimes be included in the insurance estimate given to the tenant. Check to see whether this is the case at your centre.

5. Car Parking

- Car Parking costs should normally only include line marking and other minor costs. If the amount is greater than $5000 query this cost. You should not have to pay for the costs of asphalting the car park every few years as this is a capital cost.
- If the car park is let to a private contractor, the area of the car park should be classified as GLA and not common area. The cost of the car park becomes that of the private contractor and not the tenants of the centre.

6. Energy Costs

- Some major tenancies use substantial quantities of electricity after normal hours trading (for example cinemas, railway stations etc) and are often charged separately for this by the lessor. Check that any reimbursement by these operators is deducted from your total energy costs before it has been apportioned to you.
- Test check the tariff ratings you have been charged. You need to ensure that you are always paying the best tariff rate, particularly as shopping centres operate extensively outside normal office hours

7. Lifts and Escalators

- The energy costs to run the lifts and escalators are usually determined on an "allocated basis" by the lessor from the total electricity costs. The same principles apply as those on the air conditioning checklist.
- Some old leases refer to payments for lifts only. If a centre has been redeveloped and now includes escalators and travelators, you must determine whether you will accept the costs for this extended range of equipment.
- If a bank of lifts services an office tower, alongside it or part of the centre complex, query whether you should pay for these costs particularly if the offices are excluded from GLA.

8. Repairs and Maintenance

- If the centre has recently been refurbished, check for sudden increases in budgeted repairs and maintenance. Some landlords may try to apply post construction problems to repairs and maintenance outgoings.
- Investigate jumps in this cost in the year after a refurbishment, since these costs they may now include maintenance agreements on equipment previously under guarantee
- Salary costs of maintenance staff are usually included in this item. Ascertain from store management if maintenance staff have been fully occupied in that centre. If not, ask how the cost was apportioned.

9. Gardening and Landscaping

- If the gardening and landscaping outgoing includes indoor plants, ensure that the capital cost of the pots is not added to the maintenance charge.
- Periodically, check with store management whether the centre does have gardens. This will assist in testing whether the charge is reasonable.
- Some leases provide for gardening to include "areas in the vicinity of the centre". The landlord could claim that this land is future redevelopment land that must be maintained according to the council's directive. However, in many cases the cost is simply passed onto the tenant. Remember, this land is not part of the common area of the centre on which outgoings are payable.
- Ensure that any landscaping costs are not of a capital nature. The test to employ is that the cost must not enhance the value of the centre, but instead maintain the appearance of the centre.

10. Management Expenses

- See below for a more detailed analysis.

11. Miscellaneous Expenses

- If the expense is over $5000, ascertain whether this cost includes a "community charge". This outgoing charge usually attributable to say a library in the centre for example, which does not pay outgoings as per its lease, and whose outgoings are then included in the other retailer's outgoings pool.

- If this cost is excessive check whether it includes any capital costs, such as a new motor car for the centre manager.
- Some landlords purchase items as part of an operating lease or hire agreements. They then turn these costs that are not recoverable as an outgoing into recoverable expenses by using this technique. Watch out for this.
- Note that in Victoria section 41 of the Act specifically defines capital expenditure as non-recoverable from retailers "on any areas used in association with a building and plant in a building"

12. Hydraulics/ Equipment Hire

This expense cost classification is used in the main by one major property group.

- Equipment hire usually includes scissor lifts and cherry picker equipment hired for roofs and lighting repair, and are genuine outgoings.
- Be aware that this expense has now also become a dumping ground for lease back deals of shopping centre assets.

13. Outside the Lease Terms - "acceptable" Outgoings

- From time to time, a retailer may negotiate as a "trade off" for other considerations by the landlord to pay for outgoings outside the provisions of the lease.
- Ensure that all these acceptable outgoings are authorised, fully documented and maintained with lease records. Occasionally check if the circumstances that gave rise to this additional outgoing cost, have changed.

MANAGEMENT FEES

VICTORIA - BACKGROUND

Section 49 of the Retail Leases Act 2003, places a limit on the recovery of management fees from retailers who are subject to the Act.

1. Section 49 provides that this increase must not exceed CPI.
2. The landlord's budgeted outgoings charged for the year must be sent to the retailer by 31 May each year. The only CPI index available is the CPI calculation for the March quarter, which is the percentage that must be used not an estimate by the landlord.
3. Some landlords with whom this has been queried, respond by stating that it is merely a budget and the true management fees which are often a percentage of centre rentals will only be known at the end of the year. As the section is clearly applicable when "the retailer is liable to pay", it seems logical that the cap applies when the retailer starts to make payments in terms of the budgeted outgoings.
4. When the Actual management fees are determined for the year ended 30 June, as certified by the by the auditors, the CPI adjustment will be recalculated to consider the CPI for the year ended 30 June.
5. Landlords who undertake a substantial redevelopment of a shopping centre (which may entail a major increase in management fees in future years), may be disadvantaged as the Act is silent on this and the base management fee charge subject to CPI once established may not be altered till a new lease is entered into. Thus, during a major redevelopment, the landlord will endeavour to put as many existing tenants onto a new lease if possible.
6. According to Section 49(a) (ii), the management fees must exclude salaries and other administrative costs relating to the operation of that building or shopping centre. These costs are often shown by landlords on the outgoings statements as direct administration costs of the centre, for example centre management salaries, wages and expenses. In addition, there are further fees namely management fees.
7. This raises the question of what remains in "management fees"

after deducting salaries and wages and so on. Are management fees merely an arbitrary outgoing charge by the landlord to increase their revenue without them being an actual reimbursement of a cost actually incurred? Outgoings are meant to be costs that have been incurred.

8. Retailers with a retail lease where the premises are located in a shopping centre, are only liable to contribute to the outgoing of the landlord under the following circumstances:

   • If it benefits specific retail premises in the centre and that retail tenancy benefits the retailers premises
   • If Capital Costs are not recoverable.

9. Management fees may include elements of payment for:

   • Development costs of the centre.
   • Leasing fees for the first year's income for new speciality retailers.
   • Fees for marketing and management of major retailers.
   • A fee based on a percentage of the assets in a trust, where the centre is owned by a retail trust in Australia (REITS).
   • A performance fee if the trust exceeds the growth of the property index on the Australian stock exchange

   Clearly, each of these items fall outside the definition of management fees, that can be recovered under the Act as an outgoing from retailers with leases in Victoria.

The 10% prescribed amount as set out in regulation 12 of the rules of the Act would possibly require both the landlord and the auditor to show a more detailed breakdown of how these two costs are made up.

WEST AUSTRALIA

No management fees may be recovered from a tenant in West Australia. Only the cost of managing the centre, such as centre management expenses, salaries and the cost of a maintenance team, may be recovered. More and more leases in shopping centres are being negotiated on a gross deal basis plus statutory charges, thereby incorporating the management fee into the rent.

CHAPTER 24

FIT-OUT OF A RETAIL STORE

In view of covid-19 and the non-use of your existing premises, during this period tenants must try in their negotiations with landlords, to have the rent during any new refit of the premises waived entirely, or a least for the first 3 months of the lease.

If your shop is in a new centre or the redeveloped area of an existing centre, be certain that you sign a fit-out agreement with your fit-out contractor. The fit-out agreement must clearly spell out the contractor's rights and obligations to ensure these are not in conflict with those of the main builders.

All parties must be clear about the date of hand over of the store to your shopfitter, the date of practical completion, and the date of lease commencement. The dates can be confusing, so be careful.

You could be caught up in a situation where the lease commencement date is specified to be the date of practical completion of the centre or the date of the handover of the store for fitting out. In practical terms, your fit-out might take another 4 weeks which means your first rent review may be much sooner than you anticipated. (That is after 11 months trading and not 1 year later).

If you have negotiated an incentive deal with the landlord who may have contributed to your fit-out, make sure you are aware of the fittings that will remain the property of the landlord, and those that you will be entitled to remove. The taxation implications of this type of incentive are very complicated and you should discuss it with your tax adviser.

Clauses to be included in contracts or orders awarded to fit our contractors

In accepting the order from the retailer to do the fit-out, the fit-out contractor should acknowledge and confirm the following conditions appertaining to the contract awarded:

- We understand and have received confirmation from the retailer as to the date the fit out is to be completed. We further acknowledge that time is of the essence in the completion of the contract, and that the contractor has sufficient resources and manpower to complete the fit-out on time.
- The price contained in the agreement is a fixed price and any variations will only be payable with the prior agreement of the retailer, before undertaking such additional works.
- I have read the tenancy design and fit-out guide and do not believe that there are any provisions or conditions in the guide that I cannot meet. In any event I will comply except where there is a conflict.
- I agree to use only new material or as agreed with the retailer.
- I have examined the drawings and specifications, and confirm that the proposed fit out will meet such specifications and designs and will not require any further modification or variation.
- That I have sufficient contractor's insurance to meet the requirements of the agreement to lease, and not less than $20 million in public liability.
- I have read and understood the site conditions that apply to the site during my fit-out, and that I agree to comply with these provisions. Any claims arising out of a breach of such conditions, will be for the account of the fit-out contractor without any recourse to the retailer.
- The works will be carried out during normal working hours unless the landlord, in his discretion, allows access at other times.
- In the event of any disputes I undertake to abide by an architect appointed by the Institute of Architects.
- I am satisfied, that the lessor has completed its entire works as contracted for in their agreement, to lease prior to fit -out.
- I have obtained all the necessary permits consents and approvals required under law, before the retailers works are started or carried out.
- I am satisfied as to the charges to be made to the retailer regarding category one works, and will undertake to either agree to such costs

or proceed with and assist the retailer to arbitration by a quantity surveyor in term of the Retail Leases Act.

- I agree to keep the premises tidy and clean, and on completion of the works to remove all waste and debris wrappings and residual materials which result from the retailer's works.
- I will rectify all damage to the premises or the land or any part of them which are the direct or indirect result of carrying out the retailer's works.
- I agree to indemnify the retailer from any claims arising out of delays caused by, or incidental to the execution of the retailer's works.
- Any designs and intellectual rights regarding the fit-out will always remain the property of the retailer.

The document must be signed and dated.

ADMINISTERING TURN-KEY PROJECTS

More and more large retailers are turning to a method known as "turn-key" projects to finance the enormous cost of fitting out their stores. In this situation, the landlord agrees to fit out the premises up to a certain amount in exchange for an additional rental.

This means that the retailer receives a minimum interest loan and pays it back monthly by way of rental.

The amount paid back is the same each year and is not subject to rental increases.

The assets up to the amount of the turn- key costs are retained by the lessor as an asset on which they can claim depreciation over the period of the lease.

Before embarking on such a course of action, all parties should discuss this. The tax implications are quite beneficial to each party. (The Jupiter case dealing with interest in such a transaction should also be considered in this regard). You should discuss this course of action with a tax adviser.

The retailer can claim the extra rent as a tax deduction and the landlord gives the retailer what they want. He can claim back the loan by way of a tax deduction as depreciation or a lease incentive, in some cases.

This additional rent does not form part of any formula in the lease for purposes of calculating rent. The only way to control leases with this type of financing, is to ensure that the lease schedule is structured to show the normal rent as base rent and the turnkey rent as special rent. This will allow you to monitor increases and percentage rent calculations accordingly.

Note that GST will be payable on both rentals.

Taxation legislation is constantly changing and both parties should keep up to date with any taxation changes.

Post Covid-19 smaller retailers should consider this technique.

TAKING OVER THE STORE FROM THE LANDLORD READY FOR FITTING OUT

CONDITIONS FOR HAND OVER OF PREMISES

The retailer needs to include a clause in the disclosure statement, or request confirmation by the lessor that stipulates that he will only agree to take possession of the premises from the lessor as being complete and ready for fit out providing the following:

a. All lessor's works have been completed.
b. The premises are handed over with a smooth floor in a broom swept condition and with plasterboard ceilings and walls.
c. There is a supply of water and waste to a point with a basin and tap, in accordance with the design criteria.
d. The sprinkler system including the sprinkler heads are fully installed in line with the design criteria.
e. There is an electrical board with standard power in line with the design criteria.
f. The air conditioning system and air conditioning registers have been installed to fit in with the design criteria, and that the quality if air conditioning provides comfort even when the lighting exceeds 75 watts per square metre of floor area.
g. The premises are water sealed and weatherproof.

PART 2
LEASE NEGOTIATION

THE ANALYSIS OF RESPONSIBILITY IN LEASES FOR FIRE AND EMERGENCY EQUIPMENT

Landlords, particularly those of large shopping centres, are currently under extreme pressure from state governments and state emergency services to ensure that the emergency services and fire equipment within their centres complying with set standards.

- As a result of spiralling insurance costs, landlords have been pressured by risk management departments to ensure that emergency services are properly audited and maintained.

- In states like New South Wales, the Council regulations require the shopping centres provide the councils with a satisfactory Maintenance Essential Services Certificate on a six monthly basis. This certificate must relate to the centre as a whole and must encompass all tenancies.

- In Victoria, under regulation standard AS: 2293, a compliance audit of the emergency and exit lighting needs to be conducted every 6 months. This testing must be documented to check that the lighting illuminates the area, and that the battery backup operates correctly and successfully powers the emergency and exit lighting for 90 minutes. A logbook to this effect must be kept on the premises.

- Several major landlords have instituted these emergency systems compliance audits in the shopping centres that they manage. As a result, retailers may have been sent letters requesting that they comply either by doing rectification and compliance themselves or by contracting their agents, who will charge for the service. As landlords have begun formal compliance audits and retailers in their centres may have been sent letters requesting, that they adhere to their responsibility, this raises the issue of responsibility for emergency services, as required under the lease.

- Most state emergency requirements, clearly provide that the owner of the property has the ultimate responsibility for ensuring that fire-fighting equipment is installed and properly maintained. There are severe penalties if it is not.

- Most of the shopping centres run a building intelligence program that monitors emergency and exit lighting within the centre. Some major landlords have a specific outgoing charge to cover this.

- Some centres include a "stand- by equipment" charge included in their outgoings which indicates that they have this equipment in all centres. This includes, backup generators that will cut in if there is an electricity failure and will then provide emergency lighting. Other landlords probably have similar emergency equipment but do not show it separately as an outgoing's charge.

REVIEW OF ASPECTS OF LEASES OR PART OF LEASES COVERING THE FIT OUT OF THE TENANCY

A review of most retailers' leases shows the following anomalies:

- The detailed responsibility to inspect, check and pay for emergency services and equipment is often not clearly described in the leases with one or two exceptions.
- Provisions stating that the landlord is required to install fire sprinklers, build the fire wall and install the necessary fire hydrants in the centre, are often only included in the "Agreement to Lease" and retailers need to watch for this.
- Some of the centre rules attached to the leases (that in any account form part of the lease), have a provision requiring the retailer to comply with fire regulations and to pay for any costs involved.
- In some leases dealing with sprinklers that the landlord is expected to install in the premises, the provisions are stated as follows:
  "The lessor will provide automatic fire sprinklers in accordance with Australian Standard no AS 2118, to suit a clear and empty shell shop. The lessor will also install sprinklers heads within the plasterboard ceilings. Any relocation requirement will be to the lessee's cost"
- The" Lessees Works" as set out in the "Agreement to Lease", often contains a provision that the retailer is to supply and maintain fire reels and hoses in the tenancy and provide emergency lighting for exits from the store, Clearly this is the retailer's responsibility and he has an obligation to maintain these to the required standard.
- Some leases clearly state that the lessee must provide the following in its tenancy:
  "Fire protection equipment as required by the Building Code of Australia. - supply and installation of fire extinguishers as required

by the CFA. Category 2 works schedules usually define this further by providing as follows."

"Supply and Installation in accordance with AS 2.444 requirement of 1 – 2A.20BE dry powder extinguisher to be placed within 2 meters adjacent to the switchboard, or any other special firefighting equipment (e.g. fire blankets) which may be required by CFA."

- Since sprinklers which form part of the common areas, they are clearly the responsibility of the landlord. It is assumed that over the course of the year, the landlord performs the following services:

That he has a six-monthly inspection of the fire walls and that these are tagged to this effect.

That he performs a 3 monthly inspection to check that the pressure is correct in the sprinklers and that they will function in the event of an emergency.

That he checks all fire hydrant hoses and reels within the common area of the centre at least every three months to ensure than the equipment has not been vandalised, and will function in an emergency.

- These expenses related to this service by the landlord are included in the outgoing's clause of the lease. Tenants usually accept (without seeing proof), that landlords do make these inspections and tests and that the costs are shown on the outgoing's statements provided by the landlord.

- A good example to illustrate this outgoings recovery charge is the wording in a recent lease clause. It indicates that the lessor may recover from the lessee its share of:

"The cost of maintenance, repair and testing of all fire equipment including sprinkler installations, hydrants, fire extinguishers, smoke detectors and fire-fighting equipment installed by the lessor throughout the centre together with charges rendered by any authority in the supply maintenance servicing and monitoring of fire equipment and of attending to fire alarms "

- Some retailers, however, negotiate several gross leases with landlords where variable outgoings are not payable or where only statutory charges are paid. The retailer will not see such charges on any outgoings statement, nor have confirmation that the landlord has performed the tests that have been described.

- Furthermore, some leases provide that there to be at least a 500mm gap between stacked goods or products and the sprinklers. Retailers have in the past received notices from landlords indicating that they are in breach or affect the lessor's insurance.

RECOMMENDED ACTION BY RETAILER

The audit compliance of fire equipment and emergency lighting by landlords is now a fact of life for both landlords and retailers trading in shopping centres, a strip complex or in a free-standing environment.

Retailers are encouraged to engage the services of FSE or any other qualified provider, to inspect their premises to be certain that all fire hoses and reels and emergency exit lighting are functioning. The FSE or other provider needs to give them a certificate to forward to the landlord confirming that they are meeting their responsibilities under the lease.

Retailers must instruct all retail store staff not to stack products to a height, less than 500 mm from the sprinklers.

Even though most centres are smoke free, retailers may have to give consideration to the installation of smoke detectors in their tenancy.

Note that a special condition is included in your lease (not just in the agreement to lease), that spells out the lessors and lessees requirement when dealing with emergency lighting, fire doors, fire hydrants, sprinklers and fire hoses and so on, as follows:

That the landlord undertakes and confirms to the retailer that:

- Within the past 6 months the fire doors have been inspected.
- That the pressure to the sprinklers have been checked within the past three months.
- That all hoses and fire hydrants in the common area have been checked.

CHAPTER 25

THE LEASE NEGOTIATION PROCESS

It is vitally important to understand the lease negotiation process and how to secure the best possible lease. The following background information will help you to put the process of lease negotiation in context:

- The lease process usually begins with an inquiry by the retailer to the leasing department of a shopping centre or the managing agent of an empty store advertising the store to rent.

- Sometimes the lease negotiation occurs because of a retailer acquiring a business from an existing owner. In this instance the lease is already in place but there may not be a sufficient lease period left.

- Remember, the landlord usually grants a lease of five or six years in duration. The landlord does not have to renew the lease at the end of that term. So, buying a business with only a year to go on the lease does not make good business sense, as you could lose your total investment if the landlord decides not to renew the lease.

- If the retailer already has several stores and is known in the trade, the initial discussion may result from the landlord's leasing agent contacting the retailer with a view to letting the store and negotiating a lease.

- Therefore, a retailer should always be cautious, and it is essential that a retailer entering into a lease asks as many questions as possible during this initial period. The retailer should carefully take notes of the landlord's responses as this could assist later if there is a problem, or if the landlord has made representations to the retailer which are not true or accurate.

The following are a list of the possible questions you should ask about the lease. The questions should be directed to the seller of the business, the landlord or his agent.

Q1. What is the cost of rent per square metre?

Post Covid-19, this may be not the rent per square metre, but the percentage of sales payable as rent.

The rent quoted may be a gross rent or the base rent for the premises plus outgoing and marketing levy. If the latter, inquire whether the outgoings include all statutory charges.

Some shopping centre landlords exclude council rates and water from their schedule of outgoings as these may be charged directly to the retailer by the council. They are an extra occupancy cost that must be considered by the retailer.

Q2. Does the lease have at least 5 years to run until the end of the current lease term?

If possible, request an option for one or two additional lease terms. Such options should be totally unrestricted in their ability to be exercised. In view of your experience during the crisis, you should try to have the lease for 3 years with say 3 yearly options. This will allow you to get out quicker if the crisis and lockdowns reoccur.

Remember that an option once granted to a retailer cannot be removed by the landlord. Even if the retailer does not intend to exercise the option, it will be to your advantage if you are proposing to sell the business down the track.

Q3. Have the premises been surveyed, and is there a survey certificate attached to the lease?

As rent and outgoings are measured on a rate per square metre, it is vital that the area, as shown in the lease, is certified correct by a surveyor. There is more information about this point elsewhere in the book.

PART 2
LEASE NEGOTIATION

Q4. Is there a cap on the "making good provision" in the lease or will the buyer be faced with a costly removal expense for partitions and counters as well as the cost of restoring the premises to its original state?

Always take a photo of the premises at the date of handover as it will be useful when "making good" at the end of the lease term.

Q5. If the lease has an option which results in the rent being required to "go to market", ascertain what that rental on a market review is likely to be.

This may require an opinion from a valuer as to the likely market rent on a review. Valuers often use the principal of a "kerb side valuation". Though this is not a full valuation, it is highly regarded and often less costly than a full valuation.

The legislation in New South Wales and Queensland allows for an early market review in the case of the sale of the business. New retailers acquiring a business should make use of these provisions.

Q6. When was the existing lease entered?

If the lease is one that commenced before the introduction of the current State Acts that have greatly increased the protection of retailers, the retailer may be better off requesting a new lease. This will comply with the new Act in that state, instead of a variation of the existing lease.

Q7. Does any market review have a "ratchet clause"?

Ensure that any market review clause does not have "ratchet clauses". This type of clause only allows rental to rise and not fall following a review. These clauses are now illegal in all states.

Q8. Have you ensured that clauses dealing with repainting and restoration are not at fixed intervals, but as and when necessary, as mutually agreed?

Some leases require the tenant to repaint the store every three years. The cost of repainting is expensive and the retailer should request an amendment to this clause providing for *"painting of the store during the term of the lease will not be at fixed intervals, but as and when necessary as mutually agreed by both parties"*

Q9. Have you made certain that no immediate refurbishment of the store is required on assignment?

This cost should always be considered by a potential buyer in assessing the purchase price for the store.

Q10. Does the lease contain a percentage rental clause?

Note that stores in strips and stand-alone stores usually do not have percentage rental clauses.

If the retail store is situated in a Regional Shopping Centre, ascertain whether the total gross rent, comprising base rent, variable outgoings, statutory charges and marketing contribution exceeds your acceptable industry standard.

There are several publications that set out these standards along the average gross rental payments by other retailers in similar categories are making.

Also make sure that your type of business is placed in the correct category as different businesses pay different levels of rental in the same shopping centre.

As part of the negotiation process, the landlord will normally give to the lessee several documents namely:

- A disclosure statement.
- A proposed lease offer form.
- A draft copy of the lease.
- An agreement to lease.
- A copy of the lease information document as supplied by the State Government, if applicable.
- A draft plan of the proposed store.
- If the store is in a shopping centre, the landlord will provide a list of retailers.
- If you are going into a new shopping centre, you may even receive a marketing brochure of the proposed new shopping centre development.
- A fit-out guide.

TIPS DURING THE NEGOTIATION PROCESS

- Preparation is the key to the lease negotiation process.
- With the knowledge you have acuired from this book, and knowledge about the rights given to you under the Retail Tenancy Acts in the state where you are to operate your store,(if you are under the Act), you will be equipped to begin the negotiation process with the landlord or his agent.
- Do not be afraid to quote your rights to the landlord where appropriate.
- Take all emotion out of the negotiation process. Being aggressive if things are not going well is a mistake and shows weakness. Remain detached if possible.
- Think like a landlord and try to see his point of view. This will help you to work out counter arguments.
- Ascertain in advance, the true market value of the rent in that shopping centre or strip centre by seeking information from your future retail neighbour's. Retailers are usually helpful to new retailers and will probably tell you what rent they are paying.
- Tricky negotiations may require alternative solutions. Try to put forward several alternative proposals, one of which may be mutually acceptable to both parties.
- Do not simply accept responses from the landlord's solicitor as final. Do not be afraid to object and propose alternatives for consideration. Keep the process going, until you arrive at a mutually acceptable conclusion.
- Overseas retailers coming to Australia, must consider that the Australian lease negotiating process may be totally different to what is experienced in their home country. It would be advisable to use a local retail lease consultant who knows the local process, to act on the retailer's behalf.

CHAPTER 26

DISCLOSURE STATEMENTS

Current legislation in all states, has made the disclosure statement between landlord and retailer the fundamental document in ensuring transparency and proper disclosure of all facts prior to entering a lease.

Retailers must always insist on being given a lessor's disclosure statement containing all the information as described in the schedule attached to the Acts in all states. Failure to supply a disclosure statement in Victoria, allows the retailer to avoid rent payments until one is received.

Remember, that the details as contained in the statement, continue to be considered factual throughout the term of the lease and throughout the term of any renewal options contained in the original lease. If any of the information given is misleading, the retailer may recover damages.

It cannot be emphasized enough, how vital it is that you insist on all details and representations given to you by the landlord or his representative during the negotiation phase, be included in the disclosure statement.

KEY POINTS ABOUT THE NEW UNIFORM DISCLOSURE STATEMENT

The states of Victoria, New South Wales and Queensland, have agreed on a single uniform landlord disclosure statement. The statement applies in these states came into effect on 1 July 2011. Other states have introduced their own disclosure statements that do not differ from this new uniform disclosure statement

Why the change?

It was anticipated that the nationally integrated form of disclosure statement will have benefits for both tenants and landlords.

Tenants will benefit from the increased disclosure by landlords regarding certain provisions in the Retail Leases Acts. They will be better informed of their rights and obligations under the lease and thereby may make improved decisions about their business. This will also help them to decide whether they still wish to enter a lease.

Landlords will benefit from a reduced regulatory burden, particularly those landlords who own and operate shopping centres in multiple states.

However, as the Retail Leases Acts remain separate in each state, the implications and consequences of the new disclosure statement may still affect tenants differently in each of the three states.

What has changed?

The most fundamental change, is the abolition of separate disclosure statements for a shopping centre and a non-shopping centre building or tenancy. In the case of a shopping centre tenancy, additional information is required.

What has not changed?

- The new disclosure statement and lease must still be given to the tenant at least seven days before the lease is entered.
- If a tenant has not been given a disclosure statement he may give the landlord or his agent no earlier than 7 days, and no later than 90 days after entering into the lease, a written notice about the absence of a disclosure statement.
- In Victoria, the tenant may then withhold rent until the disclosure statement is given. The tenant is not liable for rent from the day on which the tenant gave notice until the day the disclosure is given.
- The tenant may terminate the lease by written notice within 7 days after receiving the disclosure notice.
- If the premises are not available for handover on the date specified in

the disclosure statement, the tenant is not liable to pay for any rent charged prior to that date.

- If any information in the disclosure statement is misleading, false or materially incomplete, or the tenant has not been given a copy of the proposed lease, then the tenant may give the landlord or his agent written notice of termination of the lease within 28 days after receiving the disclosure statement, (or the tenant being given a copy of the proposed lease, or the date the lease is entered into whichever is the latter.)

- The landlord still has the right to object to the termination of a lease on the grounds that he acted honestly and reasonably and ought to be excused for the contravention, provided that the tenant is substantially in as good a position as he would have been, if there was no contravention.

- If the lease requires the tenant to pay or contribute towards the cost of a fit-out, this provision is void if that liability was not mentioned in the disclosure statement. This is particularly relevant in the case of category one works that the landlord usually undertakes but is paid for by the tenant.

- If on assignment of the lease, the tenant asks the landlord to give him a current disclosure statement from a specified date (that is within 3 months before the statement is given). This may mean that the landlord or his agent needs to prepare a new uniform disclosure statement. The landlord or agent can still recover reasonable legal and other costs in connection with the assignment of the lease or sub lease.

- Even though you will notice that the new disclosure statement in section 14.2 allows for an outgoings under the heading of "Sinking Fund for Repairs and Maintenance," the Victorian Act provides that "a provision in a retail lease is void to the extent that it requires the tenant to make a contribution to a sinking fund for capital works".

- The Acts in the other states do allow for the creation of a "sinking fund" for future capital works that can be recovered from the tenant as an outgoing.

- If the retailers store is in a shopping centre, the retailer must be aware of the way the Act defines a shopping centre as the new statement requires additional information to be given in this case. For example, in Victoria, the Act provides that a retail shopping centre is defined as a cluster of premises that has <u>all</u> of the following attributes: -

- At least 5 of the premises are retail premises.
- The premises are owned by the same person or have (or would have if leased) the same landlord or head landlord.
- The premises are in a single building or in 2 or more buildings that are adjoining, or separated only by common areas, or other areas belonging to the owner of the retail premises, or separated only by a road.
- The cluster of premises is promoted as, or generally regarded as constituting a shopping centre, shopping mall, shopping court or shopping arcade

THE ESSENTIAL ISSUES AND SPECIFIC ITEMS A NEW RETAILER SHOULD LOOK FOR IN THE DISCLOSURE STATEMENT

The new disclosure statement has several important and detailed changes that are worth noting, namely:

1. Structures, fixtures, plant and equipment

Whereas the old Part 3, required the landlord to set out the structure, fixtures, plant and equipment and services to or in the premises provided to the tenant, which may not have been fully completed by the landlord or his agent, the new disclosure statement sets out a list of 22 items which are required to be highlighted that have been provided in the premises.

2. Services and facilities

In addition, there is a new section 1.5 that requires disclosure of services and facilities for the benefit of the premises, for example, security services, cleaning and so on.

3. Lawful planning area

Section2.1. describing the permitted use, is the same as Part 5 Section B of the old statement, except that it comes with a warning to the tenant that he should investigate whether the proposed use of the premises is lawful under relevant planning laws.

4. Right to sell goods and services

While the old lease allows the tenant to have the right to sell specific goods and services, the new disclosure statement in section 2.2 requires the landlord to answer "yes" or "no" as to whether the whole of the permitted use is exclusive to the tenant or not.

5. Car Parks

Whereas previously, the landlord had to show the total number of car parks in the centre and the number of car parking bays available for the tenants' exclusive use, the landlord now has to show the number of available spaces for customer parking.

6. Head Leases

Section 4 is new, and requires the landlord to state "yes/no", whether the premises are leases under a head lease or crown lease. If the answer is yes, the next question is whether the landlord has provided a copy of the head lease or crown lease to the tenant. In addition, section 4.1 requires the landlord to state the current term of such a lease and whether there is an option to renew the lease during which period the options will be available.

Section 4.4 requires a disclosure by the landlord as to whether the head landlord's consent is required to the proposed lease to be entered into between landlord and tenant.

7. Survey Plan

It is no longer necessary for a survey plan to be annexed to the disclosure statement.

8. Handover Date

In section 7.1.now the handover date (actual or estimated) must be shown if it is different from the date the lease commences.

9. Tenant's Works

Whereas the old disclosure statement provided for only a list of the tenant's works to be performed by the tenant at its cost before the commencement date of the lease, and during the lease term, the new disclosure statement now requires in section 8.1, a description of works to be carried out by the landlord before the lease commences.

Section 8.2 requires the landlord to provide an estimate of the expected contribution by the tenant towards the cost of the landlord's works as well as the costs in relation to any maintenance and repair outgoings that have been included in the schedule of outgoings.

Whilst not required previously, now the landlord has to state whether he has requirements about the quality and standard of the shop front and fit-out. This may be by way of a fit-out guide.

10. Requirement to provide turnover

Now the landlord must state whether the tenant is required to provide details of turnover.

11. Non recovery of specific outgoings from the tenant

Now, there is a note in the disclosure statement, informing the tenant that according to section 50 of the Victorian Act, the landlord may be prevented from claiming certain costs such as recovery of land tax. Also, under section 52 of the Victorian Act, the landlord may be prevented from claiming costs for certain repairs and maintenance.

In addition, section 41 of the Victorian Act prevents the landlord from claiming any capital costs of the building in which the premises are located. This is not the case in the other state Acts.

Renovation and Redevelopment of the Centre

Whereas previously, the landlord merely had to state whether planning approval for renovations, redevelopments or the extension of the centre had been obtained, now the landlord or his agent, must state whether at that point in time any alterations or works are planned, to the premises or building/centre including surrounding roads during the term of the lease or any other further term or terms.

12. Relocation of tenant

The new statement now requires the landlord or his agent to state the clause number in the lease that deals with the relocation of the tenant and with the demolition of the premises or centre/building where applicable.

13. Trading Hours

Landlords must now provide the core trading hours specifically relevant to the tenant (not the shopping centre/building), on a day by day basis, including trading on public holidays. Therefore, if a trader such as a pharmacist, gym or video shop, works outside the normal centre hours, this must now be stated.

This raises the question as to whether the tenants trading hours, if agreed upon, will not be subject to a late-night trading charge for hours worked outside normal centre trading hours.

There is a further clause which provides for whether the tenant is permitted access to the premises and centre/building outside trading hours, for example bakeries or butcher shops and the like.

14. Disclosure of centre turnover information and number of shops

Whereas previously, the landlord had to reveal the number of retail premises in the Centre, the new statement requires the landlord to state the number of shops.

The new disclosure statement, requires the disclosure of annual turnover figures of the centre for the previous accounting period, if collected by the lessor. The turnover will have to be declared on either a GST inclusive or GST exclusive basis, which may differ from what is often declared in shopping centre reports. This will again give tenants access to confidential information and may cause some problems in negotiation, particularly if figures show a downward trend.

The new disclosure statement requires the disclosure of information for speciality shops (in no less than three identified categories namely food, non-food, and services), for the previous accounting period and on a per square metre basis. Again, the information must be provided if collected by the landlord.

15. Expiry date of leases of tenants in premises greater than 1000 square metres

The new section 23 of the statement, requires the disclosure of the expiry date of leases of tenants of more than 1000 square meters. Although not contentious, the person completing the disclosure statement must ensure that that the expiry dates of such tenants is absolutely accurate. Any error could lead to a claim for misleading and deceptive conduct.

16. Tenancy Mix

Under new section 24, the floor plan to be provided now must in addition to showing the tenancy mix as previously, should now show common areas, trading, kiosks, and major tenants.

In the case of competitors, the old assurance by the landlord that the centre "is an ongoing entity and changes will take place from time to time", is no longer relevant in the new statement. The landlord must answer "yes or no" as to whether he assures the tenant that the current tenant mix will not be altered by the introduction of a competitor. To comply with this, landlords may have to undertake some extensive research on each category in a centre to ascertain the impact an additional tenant will have on the category.

PART 2
LEASE NEGOTIATION

17. Traffic Flow

In the new statement, details of the customer traffic flow are still required together with an attached schedule. The traffic flow over several years, may also be shown. The new statement may require lessors to ensure that the equipment used to measure traffic flows is carefully tested and monitored for accuracy. If there are inaccuracies, the lessor will need to have tried his best to ensure that the equipment has been thoroughly tested. Post Covid-19 tenants should request that traffic flow to the centre be provided monthly.

18. Casual Mall Leasing

If the centre adheres to the casual mall leasing code of practice, as determined by the Shopping Centre Council, a copy of the casual mall policy must now be included with the disclosure statement.

19. Current legal proceedings

Section 27 of the new disclosure statement, has a new requirement to disclose details of any current legal proceedings in relation to the lawful use of the premises or building/centre. However, there is no definition of either the term "lawful use" or "current legal proceedings." To comply with this section, the landlord or agent will have to provide a list of any proceedings that is ongoing between the landlord and any tenant in that centre or complex. Besides affecting the confidentiality of discussions between landlord and tenant, disputes may include claims for arrear rent or spurious disputes by a tenant.

The disclosure of such information to a new or existing tenant may affect the future relationship between the landlord and the tenant.

20. Representations during negotiations

There is now a new section 28 that must be completed dealing with any oral or written representations made by a landlord or agent during negotiations. It is important that we include any representations during the crisis.

21. Acknowledgement of receipt of disclosure statement

Section 31, requires an acknowledgement by the tenant that he has received the disclosure statement. In the two states of New South Wales and Queensland, we previously had a lessee's disclosure statement which was not applicable in Victoria. We now have uniformity in all three states.

22. Checklist and warning for tenants

The statement now comes with a warning and a checklist for all tenants who should consider nine key questions before signing the document.

- Does the planning authority allow your proposed use for the premises under planning law?
- Is the security of your occupancy affected by?
- (a) Mortgage charges or encumbrances granted by the landlord.
- (b) Rights and obligations under a head lease?
- Do the premises comply with building and safety regulations? Are the premises affected by outstanding notices by any authority?
- Could your trading be affected by disturbances or changes to the building or centre?
- Does the landlord require you to refurbish the premises regularly or at the end of the lease?
- Can the landlord end the lease early even if you comply with the lease?
- Are all the existing structures, fixtures, plant and equipment in good working order?
- Are you required to make good the premises at the end of the lease?
- Is the tenancy mix of the shopping centre (if applicable), likely to change during the term of the lease?

Failure by the landlord or his agent to have answers to all these questions may give the tenant second thoughts about entering into the lease.

23. Attachments

If applicable the following attachments must be included with the disclosure statement:

- Plan of premises
- The Head Lease or Crown Lease
- Any additional attachments

If the premises are in a retail shopping centre the following additional attachments must be included if applicable:

- A Floor Plan
- Customer traffic flow statistics
- A Casual Mall licensing policy

CHECKING THE DISCLOSURE STATEMENT AFTER THE DEAL HAS BEEN NEGOTIATED

The retailer is required to check the disclosure statement after the deal has been concluded.

All conditions contained in the statement continue to be considered factual throughout the term of the lease and throughout the term of any renewal and to options contained in the original lease. If any of the representations are misleading, the tenant may recover damages.

It cannot be emphasised enough, that you should insist on all details and representations given to you by the landlord or his representative during the negotiation phase, be included in the disclosure statement. Check all the correspondence carefully. Often concessions obtained early in the lease negotiations are not carried forward in later letters. Be aware that concessions won from the same landlord in other lease negotiations should be transferred to the current lease. Insist that they be included in the new disclosure statement and are carried forward to the lease.

If you are having the lease checked by you solicitor or consultant, ask him to check to ensure that the provisions of the disclosure statement have been carried forward to the final lease terms.

The new Act in Victoria requires a landlord to give a tenant a disclosure 14 days(previously 7days)before entering the lease.

Failure to do so, will see the commencement date delayed until 14 days have passed.

If the proposed lease contains changes compared to the previous version given to the tenant, and the landlord fails to notify the tenant of these changes, the landlord may be subject to a fine.

CHAPTER 27

MAKING A LEASE OFFER

When negotiating a lease with a landlord, the best approach a retailer can take is to acknowledge receipt of the landlord's lease offer, while preparing their own lease offer in advance. In this way, when there are further talks, instead of attempting to bargain down the landlords offer the retailers lease offer will become the basis of the discussions. The landlord is then placed in a position of trying to negotiate up from the retailer's offer.

In addition, the lease offer will be a check list for the retailer to ensure that all aspects of the negotiation have been covered.

A STANDARD LETTER OF OFFER FOR MOST SHOPPING CENTRE TENANCIES

This letter has been prepared for a pharmacy tenant but can be adapted for any retailer depending on the circumstances of negotiation.

Project Leasing Manager

Happiness Shopping Centre

P.O. Box

Melbourne

Victoria

Dear Sir/Madam

Re: Lease XYZ RETAIL STORE – Shop 12, Happiness Shopping Centre

Thank you for your letter of invitation of 10 July 2021. We have visited the centre and have reviewed the plan which you have presented us with.

As such, we would be willing to put the following proposal for consideration. to our board:

PROPOSAL

Location: Shop 1 Lower Ground Floor.

Lessee: Partners as per current pharmacy practice as of this date or a management company to be nominated.

Size: 200 square meters (subject to survey). Irrespective of the surveyed size of the premises, the rental in year one will not be more than the agreed amount.

Handover

Date: Approximately 4 October 2021

Lease Term: 5 Years and 3 months commencing 28 days after handover of the premises or commencement of trading from the store whichever is the latter, in a clean shell state condition. We require the extra three months to allow us to trade through an additional Christmas.

Option Period: 2 terms of 3 years each.

No restrictions will be accepted on the lessor exercising this option.

Base rent: $xxxxx for year 1 plus.

However, we will only pay 75% of the base rental until the following has been completed by the lessor:

- All stores are open and trading.
- All car parks are open and available for customers.
- All the lessor's works have been completed.
- The supermarket is open and trading.

Rent Reviews: CPI. for the term of the lease.

Unless the parties have agreed to a new rental, a market review will be conducted on the exercise of the option in accordance with the Retail Tenancy Act.

During the option period, rent will again increase at the rate of CPI annually from the start of the second year of such an option period.

Outgoings Promotion: As applicable to our tenancy.

Levy: 3% of base rental.

Opening Promotion: $1000 payable 14 days prior to commencement of trading.

Guarantor: The directors of the company.

Bank Guarantee: The equivalent of 2 months base rental excluding GST.

Percentage rental:

Rental: Pharmacists are legally required not to share their income with anyone who is not a pharmacist. Therefore, percentage rent will not be applicable in the lease. However, for planning purposes the lessee will undertake to provide, monthly sales figures, comprising front of shop sales plus NHS income.

Legal Costs: Each party will be expected to bear its own legal costs in respect of the lease preparation, or any ancillary documents or guarantees. The lessee will be responsible for the costs of registering the lease.

The Act applicable to the lease: The current Retail Leases Act in the applicable state

Exclusivity: A special provision is required as follows: that no more than one tenancy will be permitted to dispense pharmaceutical products (as provided for under the National Health Scheme), at the centre during the lease term and option period.

In the event of the redevelopment of the centre of more than 100 retail tenancies allowing for an additional pharmacy being permitted in the centre, then the lessee shall be entitled to the last right of refusal on the lease for such tenancy.

OR

If no exclusivity has been promised, in the event of a second pharmacy opening in the centre, our rental will be permanently reduced to 75% of the rental payable at that time.

Payments: All rental, outgoings, and promotion contributions to be payable monthly by way of EFT only. No direct debits will be acceptable.

Lessor's contribution:

Contribution: $xxxxx contribution is payable to us 7 days after presentation of our invoice (including GST).

Repayment of the contribution in the event of assignment of the lease will be as per your lease offer. However, if the approved assignee is prepared to accept the liability then no repayment will be required by the pharmacist.

Fit-out: We will supply our normal set of plans/ drawings for approval at no cost prior to proceeding with the shop fit- out.

A signage package will be provided for approval. Consulting, design, survey costs or other engineering costs will be payable by the lessee but will be capped at $X.

There will be no charge for hoardings.

Kiosks: Whilst we accept kiosks as part of a centre layout, no kiosks will be erected within 10 meters of our lease line which will affect the sightline of the premises.

Rent in Advance: The one month's rental to be paid on the signing of the lease which will be applied to the first month's rent when payable.

Pub liability insurance:

Insurance: $20m

Retail category classification:

Classification: Pharmacy

Permitted use: The operation of a pharmacy and health food shop including retail sales and services and the operation of a mini lab, as well as other goods and services as normally undertaken by a pharmacist, as determined from time to time, (such as sales of confectionary, sporting and disability aids, health shoes, wheelchairs as well as the operation of a beauty parlour or perfumery).

The premises will also be used from time to time for the operation of medical and para-medical service providers, and special medicine preparations.

Solicitor: This offer would naturally be subject to our solicitor sighting and approving the disclosure statement, lease and its terms.

Lessor's works; The premises will have sprinklers and air conditioned to a quality in accordance with the Australian air conditioning standard. The landlord shall guarantee that the premises shall be water and weather sealed at the time of entering the lease.

Lease Terms: All amendments to standard leases previously negotiated to be carried forward to the lease for this centre.

Painting : We will undertake to paint and restore the store not at fixed intervals, but as and when necessary by mutual agreement during the lease term.

Electricity: In the event of electricity been charged to us as a result of bulk buying by the lessor, the tariff charged to us will be the "best tariff rate applicable" and in accordance with current electricity regulations. The pharmacist can use its own electricity provider if it is more cost effective.

Binding agreement:

Agreement: There will be no binding agreement between the lessor and the lessee to enter into a lease, until the necessary legal documentation is drawn up and executed by all parties.

Storeroom: In the event of a storeroom being supplied, as part of the agreement, we require a licence agreement to be supplied for such storeroom to run concurrently with the lease and to terminate at the same time as the lease. No outgoings will be applicable for the storeroom.

Outposts: The landlord shall permit us to have two outposts per annum in the centre mall at the commercial rate. The timing of such outposts shall be by mutual agreement.

Relocation : Relocation of our pharmacy during the lease or option terms as a result of the total re-development of the centre, will be permitted once the Health Commission has approved such relocation, and the landlord agrees to compensate us and pay for all costs of relocation, erection and fit out of a new pharmacy as provided under the Act.

Deregulation: In the event of the deregulation of the pharmacy industry, allowing supermarkets and other retail chains to incorporate pharmacies within their stores, the lessee shall be permitted to either surrender the lease or renegotiate it at the time, the terms and conditions of the balance of the lease.

Should the above proposal be acceptable to the lessor, we would be happy to submit an amended formal lease invitation to our board of directors for approval.

The document will need to be signed and dated.

SOME ADDITIONAL TERMS THAT COULD BE INCLUDED IN LEASE OFFERS

Quite often, the parties believe that they have agreed to the commercial terms of the lease but then find that when they receive the landlord's standard lease documents there are terms and conditions contained therein which are simply not acceptable to the retailer.

To overcome this, retailers have started to put the following special conditions in their lease offers. In any event, when checking the lease, you should request that such clauses be deleted or amended. (Some of these provisions have already been dealt with previously).

Kiosks: No Kiosk (other than existing kiosks) will be permitted within 10 meters of our lease line which will affect the view of our store or impair ingress or egress from our store.

Directors Guarantees: If the retail store is a company, no director's guarantee, or bank guarantees will be provided by the lessee.

Method of payment of rent: The payment of rent and outgoings will be. by electronic transfer and not by direct debit.

Opening promotion levy: If the tenancy is to be in a new shopping centre and there is to be a "once off" opening promotion levy, this levy must be payable 14 days before the commencement of trading from the store. In addition, the lessor will provide details within 3 months of opening on how the opening promotion contributions have been spent.

Consulting Fees: The retailer will not be responsible for the payment of any consulting, plan approval or engineering costs in respect of the fit out.

CPI rent increases: If rent increases are to be on the basis of CPI plus a fixed percentage which is permitted in all states except Victoria, we require a provision that if CPI is negative, that rent will fall on the anniversary date of the lease.

Outgoings: If we do a deal based on net rent plus outgoings and the deal is say for less than 1 year (which in some states would take us outside the Act), irrespective of whether we fall under the Act or not, we must make the following lease provision:

- In the case of stores in Queensland, South Australia and Victoria, land tax is not recoverable as an outgoing from tenants.
- In the case of West Australia, management fees are not recoverable as an outgoing from tenants.
- In the case of Victoria, management fees may not increase by more than CPI annually.

Tenancies in strip centres: If the retailer is opening a retail store in a strip centre that may be subject to flooding from storms, we must provide that the lease contains a condition requiring the landlord to agree that on the handover of the premises to the tenant that the premises are water and weather sealed.

Insurance: The following provisions should be included:

- Public liability insurance will be taken out to an amount of $20m, and in addition the retailer will only keep an industrial special risks policy.
- The company's insurance policies are to be in the name of the retailer and the lessor's interest only will be noted in the policy.
- No policy will be taken out by the lessee in respect of limitation of the landlord's liability in the event of a claim.

Fit-out contributions: If you have negotiated an incentive deal with the landlord who may have contributed to the fit-out, the following provision in the lease is required; that the fittings making up the contribution will remain the property of the landlord for the term of the lease, but the retailer may or may not remove them at the end of the lease term. The taxation implications of this type of incentive are overly complicated, and you should first clear this with your tax adviser.

In the case of a fit-out contribution which includes a "claw back" provision, there must be a provision in the lease stating that in the event of a relocation to an assignee acceptable to the lessor, no repayment of the fit out contribution will be required by the tenant retailer, provided that the assignee is prepared to accept this contingent liability.

Cost of hoardings during fit-out: All costs of hoardings during the fit-out store will be payable by the lessor.

Painting and restoration during the lease term: Painting and restoring of the premises during the lease term and option periods, will occur as and when necessary by mutual consent and not as decided by the landlord unilaterally.

Quality of air conditioning to be provided: You must request a provision in the lease to ensure that "*The lessor shall provide air conditioning to the premises of a quality so as to provide comfort conditions even when the lighting heat intensity exceeds 50 watts per square metre of the floor area of the demised* *premises including other heat producing equipment within the premises"*. This is in accordance with the Australian standard.

Fire walls sprinklers and emergency lighting: We require a provision in the lease or confirmation from the landlord, that irrespective of these costs being included in the definition of outgoings in the lease, and that the landlord agrees to ensure the following:

- That the landlord will conduct a six-monthly inspection of the fire walls, and these will be tagged to this effect.
- That the landlord will conduct a 3 monthly inspection to check that the pressure to the sprinklers in your tenancy is correct and that they will function in the event of an emergency.
- All fire hydrants hoses and reels within the common area of the centre are also checked at least every 3 months, to ensure than the equipment has not been vandalised and will function in an emergency.

Change of signs and colour: We require a general provision that no permission will be required from the lessor in the event of a total change of corporate colour or image change of the entire network.

Restoration of the shop-front during lease term: There should be provision in the lease that this will only be required and not at fixed intervals, but as and when necessary, if mutually agreed to by both parties.

Services: In the event of electricity or gas being provided by the lessor to the premises, this will be charged at the same tariff rate as paid by the landlord or at the best rate. In addition, the retailer will be able to acquire such services from their own providers.

Relocation: A section of the lease offer must include the following:

- That the alternative premises offered will be in a position in the centre which is no worse than the position the lessee currently enjoys.
- The rental will be at the same rental as the current lease adjusted, to take into account the commercial value of the new premises at the time of relocation, as agreed by the parties, or in the absence of agreement, as determined by a valuer appointed by the Small Business Commissioner (in the case of Victoria).

- The lessor will in addition, agree to waive the "making good" and decommissioning costs of the existing premises and pay for any surrender of lease legal costs.

Market reviews in Victoria: In Victoria, if there are to be market reviews on an exercise of the option in the lease; ensure that there is a provision in the lease for the market review to be completed first before you have to exercise your option. Other States, have the timetable the right way around (namely, that we have the review first, then the right to exercise the option). This is not the case in Victorian legislation.

Lease Term: Should the date of commencement of trading be delayed because of the late handover of the premises prior to fit out, then the commencement date and the termination date will be adjusted accordingly.

Storeroom: In the event of a storeroom being supplied as part of the rental, request a licence agreement to be supplied for the storeroom to run concurrently with the lease and to terminate at the same time as the lease.

New shopping centres:

Gross rental for the new tenancy will be limited to a percentage of sales until such time as the centre is completed. The centre shall be deemed to be completed when all the following have occurred:

- All majors are trading.
- Car parking is 100% complete.
- 95% of the specialty areas are trading or malls to be substantially complete.

Cap on sales to dissolve the lease:

We need a provision in the lease that if sales do not reach a specific level of sales by the end of year 2, then the tenant will be entitled to cancel the lease.

CHAPTER 28

PURCHASING A NEW STORE AND TAKING OVER AN ASSIGNMENT OF THE LEASE FROM THE EXISTING TENANT, OR ASSIGNING YOUR LEASE TO A NEW OPERATOR

When a retailer takes over a store from another tenant, or the retailer plans to sell a store to another retailer, his understanding of the lease implications, are essential.

It is therefore imperative that when you are thinking about a possible sale of your business that you ensure that your "lease is in order". Remember, that the lease is one of the key pillars on which your negotiations with the purchaser, is based. The quality of the lease could either break or make your sale.

WHAT SHOULD THE SELLER TAKE INTO ACCOUNT?

There are two major considerations for a retailer to consider:

- Do I have a good retail lease that will ensure I can maximize its value in the event of a sale of the retail store?

- What is my position when the lease is up for renewal, but it contains no further option?

Note, that at present it would be difficult for the landlord to accept a higher rental from another retailer and simply evict you.

If for instance, you are a pharmacist, under the Guild/ Government Agreement you may have some protection preventing another pharmacy taking up your vacated space. It is important in your lease negotiation, that you are aware of this.

If you lose you premises you may still be able to save the value of your goodwill by relocating outside the shopping centre to a strip centre. However, the ability to achieve this is hard to predict, and each case will be different.

WHAT WILL A BUYER BE LOOKING AT IN THE LEASE WHEN CARRING OUT A DUE DILLIGENCE ON THE PURCHASE OF YOUR STORE?

In arriving at the final selling price, it would be prudent for a potential buyer to carry out a proper due diligence on the lease underpinning the purchase of the store. There may well be several provisions contained in the lease that need to be considered in the final purchase price

These include:

Does the lease provide for a refit of the premises at the end of the current lease term? If it does, the purchaser may have to spend $100000 to $150000 of his own funds, within a short while of taking over the store. This may mean that an appropriate sum of money may have to be deducted from the purchase price.

Given the flat retail conditions in some shopping centers, the store may have been enjoying a marketing or rental abatement of about $2500 per month being credited to the monthly statement. This will mean, that the rental paid as per the profit and loss presented could be understated. (Often these rental abatements will cease on assignment). Such credits should be added back and deducted from the profit of the business.

Many leases provide for the painting of the premises every 3 years. This may well cost up to $5000 for the painting. If the date for painting has not yet been reached before the takeover, a sum equivalent to the above should be considered in the purchase price.

If you are buying a store in a rising rental market, and the lease calls for a market review, which is to take place after the new buyer has taken over, the purchaser may well have to ask for an independent valuer's opinion of what this may be. A substantial increase in the market rental will affect the future profitability of the business and should be considered when determining the profitability on which a return on investment will be calculated.

Leases often provide for several months' rental payment into the center's promotion fund on the assignment of the lease. Who is to pay this assignment fee needs to be negotiated by the parties?

In addition, some leases provide that on assignment of the lease there is to be an automatic market review. Again, you should ensure that you obtain an independent valuer's opinion of what this is likely to be. This should be considered in determining the profitability of the business.

It is important to ascertain the "vintage" of the lease. If the lease is old and is currently in the second option period, you may well be stuck with all the old provisions of the various State Acts. This could be disadvantageous to a new buyer. It may well be a negotiating point for the buyer to rather negotiate a new lease than live with a "bad old lease"

If the business is in an old centre that is likely to be refurbished or upgraded shortly, there may be certain outgoings such as building maintenance, air conditioning being upgraded, or a new centre owner substantially increasing management costs. These factors, could cause an increase in future outgoings costs. You need to take this into account in assessing the realistic future occupancy costs of the store.

All leases provide for a "make good provision" at the end of the lease. If the store has been restructured to suit the needs of the current occupier, it may cost a substantial amount to put the store back to its original condition.

If possible, always request whether there were photos of the store at the date of hand over. Comparing old and current photos, will allow the purchaser to ascertain what the potential liability will be for making good at the end of the lease.

New legislation in some states requires the person assigning the lease to provide a new disclosure statement on the centre. Make sure that you ask for this, as it will provide you details of any future developments of the centre, that may result in some disruption to trading while this redevelopment takes place.

If there is an "exclusivity provision" in the lease as to the number of similar businesses that may operate in a centre, make sure that this provision continues assignment of the lease.

PART 2
LEASE NEGOTIATION

CHAPTER 29

THE RIGHTS OF FRANCHISEES AND FRANCHISORS UNDER THE STATE RETAIL LEASES ACTS

In Australia, the franchisee, and the franchisor both have rights and obligations under State as well as Federal legislation. In this chapter, we will look at their State rights, and in the following chapter their Federal rights.

STATE LEGISLATION – VICTORIA

Victoria is the most progressive of all the states in its dealing with retail tenancy legislation and the way in which it affects landlords, franchisees, and franchisors.

SUMMARY OF THE VICTORIAN FRANCHISE LEGISLATION

The material in this chapter does not quote the act in its entirety. However, the following points summarises a franchisee's position:

- The provisions of the Act apply in the case of the franchisor entering a current lease with the landlord for premises.
- Franchisors as part of the franchising process, normally enter a single unit franchise occupancy licence agreement. This allows the franchisee to occupy the premises leased by the franchisor from the

landlord for the purpose of establishing and conducting the franchise operation.

- The franchisor, normally requires the franchisee to pay the landlord the rent, outgoings, security deposit and any other requirement of the lease.
- The franchisee, is also obligated to observe all the covenants of the lease imposed on the franchisor.
- The franchisee, must acknowledge that the terms of the lease will be adhered to as if it were the lessee.
- The franchisee, acknowledges that where there is any inconsistency between the lease and the licence agreement, the lease will prevail.
- The franchisee, agrees to have read the lease and is familiar with its terms.

These details may at times seem unnecessary reading or time consuming, but as always in negotiations, it is necessary to understand the "small print".

The arrangements between the franchisor, franchisee and landlord are affected by the inclusion of the new provisions in the Victorian act in the following way:

1. UNDER THE ACT THE LANDLORD MAY RESERVE THE RIGHT TO REFUSE A SUB-LEASE OR MORTGAGE

Section 63 of the new Act, stipulates that a retail premises lease may contain a provision allowing the landlord the absolute discretion to refuse to consent to the following:

- The granting of a sub-lease, licence or concession in respect of all or part of the retail premises.
- The parting with occupancy rights to all, or part of the premises.
- The franchisor mortgaging or otherwise encumbering the franchisor's estate, or interest in the lease. This last provision, if it becomes general practice, may in future make it impossible for franchisors to grant franchises. It may also hamper the franchisee's ability to finance their fit-outs by a mortgage of the lease.
- Franchisors, who propose to establish a franchise in premises where franchisees may use the lease as security for finance, are best off

negotiating the terms in their leases to enable them to manage the franchise.

- Section 63 allows the landlord to become an active party to the franchise occupancy licence arrangement, both as to the vetting of the agreement and charging of a fee for this involvement.

2. KEY MONEY AND GOODWILL PAYMENTS PROHIBITED

Section 23 of the Act provides that "key-money" is prohibited. Any form of payment by a retailer to a landlord, or any consideration for the goodwill of any business carried on in the premises is forbidden.

However, various other payments, that do not constitute rent, but are valid, are also set out in this section. These include rent in advance, bonds, security deposits and guarantees. They even include, seeking and accepting payment for the grant of a franchise in connection with the lease being granted.

Even more important from a franchising point of view, section 23(3) specifically provides that the landlord may recover reasonably incurred costs from the retailer, incurred in investigating a proposed assignee of the lease or sub-lessee of the premises (which the licence agreement confers).

Under the State Act both the licence agreement and details of the franchisee is now permitted to be vetted by the landlord.

There appears to be no limit to the amount that can be recovered beyond what is reasonable. Since legal costs are no longer recoverable from retailers under the Act in Victoria, this cost may be a way of recovering these expenses.

3. DISCLOSURE STATEMENTS BETWEEN FRANCHISOR AND FRANCHISEE

If a franchisor proposes to grant a licence to a person to use all or part of the retail premises, wholly or predominantly for the carrying on of the business, under a name or identifying mark, commonly associated with or controlled by the retailer, or a person or corporation connected with the franchisor, then the franchisor must supply the proposed licensee *within 7 days before* the grant of the licence. The following procedures must be followed:

- A copy of the disclosure statement must be given to the franchisee concerning the lease. Failure to provide a disclosure statement may attract a penalty of $1000 or 10 penalty points.
- As the disclosure statement has been given to the franchisee, any changes that the franchisor is aware of, or could reasonably be expected to be aware of, that may have affected the information in the disclosure statement must now be disclosed to the franchisee.
- It is therefore essential that the occupancy licence agreement contains a provision that the "franchisee acknowledges that he or she has received the disclosure statement within 7 days of signing of the licence agreement".
- The franchisor will need to receive a new disclosure document from the landlord to give to the franchisee. Sufficient time needs to be allowed for receipt of the disclosure statement from the landlord.
- The franchisor must decide whether he wishes to have the franchisee under the Act or not. If not, this may conflict with the franchising code.
- If the lease is entered into between the landlord and the franchisee, the lease will automatically apply to the franchisee as if he were the tenant.
- If the lease is entered into between the franchisor and the landlord, and the franchisor enters into a licence agreement with the franchisee, such a licence agreement will now have to be approved by the landlord.
- Disputes between the franchisor and the franchisee in relation to the premises will be treated as part of the overall franchising relationship. They will be subject to the provisions under the Trade Practices Act.

This is a complicated section in the Act and needs to be fully understood by any person acting on behalf of either for the franchisee or the franchisor.

PART 2
LEASE NEGOTIATION

SOUTH AUSTRALIA AND WEST AUSTRALIA

The states of South Australia and West Australia have introduced franchising bills to examine the State regulation of franchising. Franchisees contemplating the purchase of a franchise in these states need to check the progress of these bills before signing any documents.

CHAPTER 30

THE RIGHTS OF FRANCHISEES AND FRANCHISORS UNDER THE FEDERAL FRANCHISING CODE OF CONDUCT

FEDERAL LEGISLATION

The federal legislation governing franchising is contained in an act known as the Competition and Consumer (Industry Codes- Franchising) Regulations 2014. Select Legislative Instrument No 168 2014.

Every franchisee or proposed franchisee needs to obtain a copy of the Code either from the franchisor or from the Office of Drafting and Publishing Attorney-General's Department Canberra.

The old regulations and Code have been substantially overhauled and a new franchising code of conduct has now been enacted by Parliament. I do not intend to present all the details contained in the Code. This should be read in detail by any proposed franchisee however I have highlighted the main points that franchisees need be aware of prior to entering into negotiations.

WHAT DOCUMENTS ARE REQUIRED TO COVER A FRANCHISE ARRANGEMENT?

The fundamental documents in any franchise arrangement are as follows:

- A copy of the franchise agreement, in the form it is to be executed.
- A disclosure statement.
- A copy of the code.

The disclosure statement must be given at least 14 days before the franchisee either enters into the franchise agreement or pays any non-refundable money in advance to the franchisor or his agent or associate. The franchise disclosure statement must be given to a franchisee if the franchisee is proposing to renew or extend the term of the franchise agreement.

If the franchisee makes a written request for a disclosure statement, the franchisor must provide the franchisee with a current disclosure statement within 14 days of the request. Remember, that a franchisee can request a disclosure statement only once in any 12-month period.

WHAT ARE THE FUNDAMENTAL CONDITIONS OF A FRANCHISE AGREEMENT?

The Code prescribes the following specific conditions that must be included in all franchise agreements:

A cooling off period:

- A prospective franchisee is entitled to a cooling off period of seven days after entering into a franchise agreement (this is not the case of a renewal extension or transfer of the franchise) or making any payment under the agreement whichever occurs earlier.
- If the franchisee terminates the agreement during the cooling off period, he is entitled to a refund of all payments less any reasonable franchisor's expenses (which must be described fully in the agreement) within 14 days.

Membership of franchise associations

- The franchisor is prohibited from preventing franchisees forming an association with other prospective franchisees for a lawful purpose. However, it is unlawful for franchisees to meet to make a contract or arrangement or arrive at an understanding for the purpose of fixing, controlling, or maintaining the price that they will charge for goods and services.

General release from liabilities

- A clause which prohibits the inclusions of any general "release from liabilities" by the franchisor, or the release of waivers of representations" is given to the franchisee by the franchisors during negotiations is not acceptable.

Franchisees right to transfer or novate a franchise agreement

A franchisee always has the right to transfer or novate a franchise agreement. This request must be in writing and the franchisor may not unreasonably withhold consent.

- The franchisor can only withhold consent in the following circumstances:

  1. If the transferee is unlikely to meet the financial obligations of the agreement.
  2. If the transferee does not meet a particular requirement of the agreement.
  3. If the transferee does not meet the franchisor's selection criteria.
  4. If the transfer will have an adverse effect on the franchise system in general.
  5. If the transferee does not agree in writing to comply with the obligations under the franchise agreement.
  6. If the franchisee has breached the franchise agreement and has not remedied the breach.

- Franchisors will under the new regulations be able to request certain information from an existing or current franchisee before they agree to transfer, or the novation of the franchise agreement. The franchisee is deemed to have consented to the transfer or novation if he does not object to the transfer within 42 days of the written notice.
- Whilst the franchisor has the right to exercise his discretion in

PART 2
LEASE NEGOTIATION

objecting to a transfer or novation, he may not be permitted to act unconscionably in the exercise of his discretion.

Renewal of the agreement when it expires

- The franchisor is not obliged to renew the franchise agreement when it expires unless there is an option for a further period, and the franchisee exercises the option as per the requirements of the agreement.
- If the agreement runs for more than 6 months, the franchisor must notify the franchisee at least 6 months before the end of the term of the franchise agreement as to whether it will be renewed or not. If it is to be renewed, the franchisee must then enter into a new agreement with the franchisor.
- If the agreement has been made for less than 6 months, then 1 months' notice is required.

Termination of the franchise agreement

- The franchising Code sets out specific requirements where parties seek to terminate a franchise agreement. These essentially cover 3 circumstances:-

    1. Where the franchisee has breached the franchise agreement.
    2. If special circumstances apply in the Code that permits the franchisor to terminate the agreement.
    3. Where the franchisee has not breached the agreement, but the franchisor seeks to terminate the agreement in accordance with its terms, but without the consent of the franchisee to its termination.

- In the first case where the franchisee seeks to terminate the agreement due to the breach of the agreement, the franchisor must give the franchisee 30 days' notice in writing, of his intention to terminate the agreement. The franchisor must stipulate exactly what needs to be done to remedy the breach.
- If the breach is remedied within the prescribed time frame, the

franchisor can no longer proceed with the termination unless there are special circumstances. These circumstances are listed as follows:

1. If the franchisee no longer holds a licence required to carry on the franchise. For example, in the case of a liquor retail franchise, where the franchisee has lost his liquor licence.
2. If the franchisee becomes bankrupt or insolvent, puts his affairs under administration or if his company is deregistered by the Australian Securities and Investments Commission.
3. If the franchisee voluntarily abandons the franchise.
4. If the franchisee is convicted of a serious offence.
5. If the franchisee operates the franchise in a way that endangers public health or safety.
6. If the franchisee is fraudulent in connection with the operation of the franchise.
7. If the franchisee and franchisor mutually agree to the termination of the agreement.

- If the franchisor decides to terminate the agreement, without the franchisees consent, having given proper notice of his intentions, the franchisee has the right to use the dispute resolution procedure as contained in Part 4 of the Code.
- The new Code provides for a statement in the agreement of the franchisee's rights at the end of the term. This includes prescribed wording that must be used, depending on whether the franchisee has a right to extend, a right to renew or neither of those rights.

Leases and Licence agreements

Usually the agreement includes a copy of the lease for the premises, and or any licence agreements given to the franchisee for the right to occupy the premises.

Sometimes franchise lease arrangements are complicated and tricky. For instance, the lease maybe in the name of the franchisor and the franchisee is expected to be responsible for paying the rent directly to the landlord. He may also be required to give the landlord a "back to back" guarantee in respect of the bank guarantee the franchisor gave to the landlord in support of the lease. In other cases, the lease is in the name of the franchisee, who is responsible for paying the rent and providing the bank and other guarantees

In other chapters of this book we examine the negotiation of leases and the requirements of landlords in respect of leases. We also look at situations where franchisees, sell the business and then has to go through the process of assigning the lease to a new franchisee.

Act in Good Faith

The new Code provides that parties to a franchise agreement," must act towards another party with good faith". This obligation applies to any dealing or dispute relating to the agreement as well as the negotiation of the agreement. Franchise agreements cannot limit or exclude this obligation.

A party may be liable for a civil penalty if it breaches this obligation.

Responsibilities before entering into the franchise agreement

This obligation in respect of pre-contractual negotiations and dispute resolution extends the common law position. For both parties it creates a perspective as to what constitutes good faith during negotiations.

Before a franchisor can enter into, renew or receive a non-refundable payment relating to a franchise agreement, the franchisor must obtain a written statement from the prospective franchisee that they have received, read and had a reasonable opportunity to understand the disclosure statement and code.

The franchisor may not enter into a franchise agreement, unless he has received a statement signed by the prospective franchisee, confirming that he has been given advice about the proposed franchise agreement by an independent legal adviser, business adviser or accountant or have been told that they should obtain advice from an adviser, and has decided not to seek it.

Marketing and advertising fees

The new Code requires franchisors to keep a separate bank account for marketing and advertising fees. The Code expects franchisors to pay the fees on the same basis as other franchisees for franchisor operated stores. The purpose of this amendment to the Code is to increase greater equality in relation to marketing funds.

Post term restraints of trade

Many franchisors, who included in past franchise agreements post-termination restraints, will be greatly affected by the new amendments to the Code. Franchisors will be forced to pay for the protection afforded by such restraints if they decline a franchisee's request to renew their franchise agreement.

As a result of the above amendment, any restraint of trade clause in a franchise agreement will not be enforceable in the following situations:

- If the franchisee wishes to have the franchise agreement renewed on similar terms.
- If the franchisee is not in breach of the agreement.
- If the franchisee abides by all the confidentiality clauses in the agreement and does not infringe the intellectual property of the franchisor.
- If the franchisor does not renew the franchise agreement and either the franchisee claimed compensation (but the compensation given was only a nominal amount and did not genuinely compensate the franchisee or the agreement did not allow the franchisee to claim compensation).

Dispute Resolutions

- The Code provides that if either party refers a dispute to a mediator, both the parties must attend the mediation and try to resolve the dispute.
- A party is thought to be attempting to resolve the dispute if they carry out the following actions:

  1. Attend and participate in meetings at reasonable times.
  2. At the beginning of the mediation process, make their intentions clear as to what they are trying to achieve.

PART 2
LEASE NEGOTIATION

3. Observe any confidentiality agreements.
4. Do not damage the reputation of the franchise system.

- The parties to a dispute are equally liable for the costs of mediation unless they agree otherwise.
- The costs of mediation include the cost of the mediator, room hire and any expert reports that may be required, as agreed upon by the parties.
- The new Code also provides for a new dispute framework that will allow for disputes to be dealt with by an internal dispute resolution procedure. This allows parties the flexibility of not having to go to mediation. However, either party still has the right to insist on attending a mediation session.
- Franchisors may not include a clause in the franchise agreement that requires mediation or litigation to take place outside the state or territory in which the franchised business is based.
- Franchise agreements under the new Code, cannot include a clause requiring franchisees to pay for any costs of settling any dispute under the agreement.

DISCLOSURE STATEMENTS

WHAT ARE THE MAIN ISSUES COVERED BY THE DISCLOSURE DOCUMENT?

As indicated, after the franchise agreement, the disclosure statement is the second most important document in any franchise arrangement between a franchisor and a franchisee.

Information contained in the disclosure statement provides the basis for thoroughly analyzing the potential for a franchise. It establishes whether the franchisee will have the expertise to run such a business successfully It is also allows the franchisee the opportunity to investigate the franchisor with whom he is about to "get married "to for 5 years or more, and to determine whether all the information contained in the statement is truthful and accurate.

Franchisors will under the new Code, be required to provide the franchisee with a short summary of key risks called an Information Statement for a prospective franchisee The layout of this statement is included in Annexure 2 of the Code. This statement should be provided as soon as practicable after the prospective franchisee formally expresses an interest in acquiring a franchise business.

The following specific points, (including the new amendments) in the disclosure statement, needs to be looked at and to be investigated in detail by any proposed franchisee before entering into any agreement:

Compulsory Information in Disclosure Statements

The following information in terms of the Code must be included in the disclosure statement:

- Details of the number of franchises in operation.
- Information about existing franchises including locations, contact details and when each franchise was started.
- Information about past franchise businesses, including the number of businesses transferred, those terminated, bought back or not renewed in the last three financial years.
- Details of any litigation involving directors or associates of the franchisor.
- Disclosure of master franchise details.
- Information in relation to online sales. The franchisor must disclose the respective rights of the franchisor and franchisee to conduct and benefit from online sales. This includes any ability or intention of the franchisor to conduct online sales.
- The franchisor must include details about the possibility to renew. If this is not stated, the franchisee will be entitled to compensation. The new Code prescribes a specific way of writing to be used in the disclosure statement when there is no right of renewal.
- In the disclosure statement, the new Code requires a full statement about the rights of the franchisee concerning extending, renewing, or neither of these rights. The Code prescribes specific wording to be used for this.
- Information about the relevant experience of each officer of the franchise.

- Information about the relevant business experience of each officer of the franchisor.
- The name of the agent to whom payments must be made.
- The financial stability and business reputation of the franchisor. If not mentioned in the disclosure statement, the franchisor must disclose" materially relevant" facts within a reasonable time or not more than 14 days of the franchisor becoming aware of these facts including the following:

    1. A change in the franchisor's majority ownership.
    2. Details of criminal and civil legal proceedings involving the franchisor.
    3. An award in arbitration against the franchisor.
    4. Insolvency of the franchisor.
    5. The existence and content of undertakings or orders against the franchisor.

- Details about the site and territory.
- The franchisor must describe the area occupied in the agreement. This may include a specific shop in a shopping centre or the whole suburb containing the shopping centre. If it was occupied by a previous franchisee, reasons must be given as to why the previous franchisee ceased to operate.
- Details of the exclusivity or non-exclusivity of nominated territory.
- Types of training and other assistance offered to the franchisee.
- Details of franchisee's requirements for the supply of goods or services.
- Financial arrangements and future profitability of the franchise.
- The conditions of financing arrangements as offered by the franchisor.
- Earnings information about the franchise based on reasonable grounds.
- Any obligations for the franchise to enter into other agreements such as leases, subleases, hire purchase agreements or security agreements.
- Establishment costs of the business.
- Details of intellectual property, including trademarks, patents, designs or copyright.
- Details of any marketing or other cooperative funds controlled by the franchisor.

MATTERS ARISING FROM THE RECEIPT OF THE DISCLOSURE STATEMENT TO BE CONSIDERED BY THE FRANCHISEE, OR TO BE DISCUSSED WITH HIS ADVISORS AS PART OF THE NEGOTIATION

Each point that refers to the disclosure statements needs to be carefully evaluated in the light of the following practical considerations:

The number and experience of existing Franchises

- The number of franchises provide some measure of stability and experience of the franchisor. A franchisee's risk may be reduced when he selects a franchisor with many franchisees.
- Equally important is the number of franchise operations that have been closed or repurchased by the franchisor. If these are a large number, this usually means that there have been problems in the past. The more franchises that have experienced problems the greater is the risk in purchasing a business.
- Talk to some of the current franchisees, and in particular, past ones who can offer a unique insight into franchisor's behavior and the service provided to franchisees.
- A franchisee should not be afraid to ask other franchisees whether the actual profit they make each year equaled the amount that the franchisor told them to expect.
- The experience of both the management and directors of the franchisor is critical to the competence of the franchisor. The franchisor should have sufficient experience to add to your business functioning. They should also have knowledge and understanding about the type of business operation they are selling. The length of their experience often indicates stability and a higher potential for franchises to succeed in the future.

Health of the Franchising Operation

The potential franchisee should request a copy of a certified financial statement from the franchisor that indicates a financially healthy organization. In addition, taking out a Dun and Bradstreet credit report on the franchisor is useful as it could bring to light any ongoing litigation against the franchisor.

Territory covered by the Franchise

A territory may be defined as a suburb, a city or even just a particular shopping centre. Therefore, the franchisee should know his exact boundary. It is important that the franchisee has exclusivity to that territory defined in the statement.

Supply of product

- Ascertain whether the franchisee will be offered the right to be supplied with the entire range of products sold by the franchisor. In addition, find out whether you can buy product direct from suppliers who are approved by the franchisor.
- Ascertain if you are required to maintain a level of inventory.
- Ascertain whether you have the right to return goods once purchased.
- Inquire from the franchisor if he or his associate will receive a rebate or financial benefit from the supply of goods or services, and whether such rebates are shared directly or indirectly with franchisees.

Training

- One of the most important services offered by the franchisor is training. The amount of training that you receive can be critical to your success. The best training programs will include a combination of classroom training and on the job training. There should be at least a few weeks training for it to be effective.
- There must be a large amount of assistance provided with the startup of the business. This is the most difficult period and requires a great deal of support. There should be continued help offered on a regular basis as well as during any unexpected crises. For example, in the situation where the franchisee takes ill and cannot operate the franchise for some time.
- The franchisee should inquire whether the franchisor will supply a franchise manual setting out how the franchise model and all its

operations are to operate. The manual should describe how to use it to best settle into the franchise.

Franchise fees and other financial costs

- The franchise fee and the capital costs of establishing the business are the biggest obstacles for most potential franchisees. Once you establish your own net worth, discuss with your banker the amount of money you can borrow.
- Determine from the franchisor what assistance he can provide for financing your business. This may include the costs for the franchises fee, equipment, supplies and operating capital. If this is to be in the form of an agreement, make sure that you carefully examine the interest rates and loan conditions. Always have the entire document checked by your financial adviser.
- Determine how long the franchise is expected to operate and if there will be sufficient revenue to cover expenses. This will help you to calculate the amount of funding that you will need to cover any deficit.
- If the franchisee is required to make a payment before the franchise agreement is entered into, the franchisee should ascertain why the money is required, how the money is to be used, who will hold the money and the conditions under which a payment will be refunded.

Marketing or other cooperative funds

If the franchisee is required to contribute to a marketing fund controlled by the franchisor, the franchisee needs to ask the following questions:

- Who else contributes to the fund, for example, the franchisor or an outside supplier?
- How much does the franchisee contribute, and whether other franchisees contribute at a different rate?
- Who controls and administers the fund?
- Is the fund audited? if so by whom? How can the funds financial statements be inspected?
- What type of expenses will the fund be used for?

- Does the fund contribute to the goods and services of the franchisor or its associates?
- Is the franchisor required to spend part of the funds in advertising or promotion of the franchisee's own business?

OTHER NEW AMENDMENTS TO THE CODE

As mentioned earlier, the federal government recently implemented a series of major changes to the Code as well as reinforcing some existing provisions. These changes were made with the express benefit of assisting franchisees, and to give confidence to those considering entering the sector. They include the following:

GENERAL

- More disclosure information by the franchisor at the start of the franchise including a simpler disclosure statement. Any new franchisee must ensure that he receives this new disclosure statement which is much more transparent than previously.
- A disclosure statement must now provide that like any business, the franchise or the franchisor can fail, and this could have consequences for the franchisee.
- Franchisors will be required to give franchisees six months' notice if they do not intend to renew a franchise agreement. If the term of the franchise is less than 6 months, then only one month's notice is required.
- Franchisors will be required to disclose to all prospective franchisees more information on unilateral contract negotiations or confidentiality obligations.
- Franchisors must also disclose whether there are any requirements for the franchisee to pay a franchisor's legal costs incurred in a dispute resolution.

VARIATIONS TO PAST AND FUTURE FRANCHISE AGREEMENTS

- Franchisors are required to disclose the circumstances in which they may unilaterally vary the franchise agreement in the future.

END OF LEASE TERM AND FRANCHISE AGREEMENTS

Franchisors are required to disclose any details of the arrangements that will apply at the end of the lease term including the following:

- Whether the franchisee will have any options to renew the franchise, extend the scope of the franchise agreement or enter into a new agreement. If so, what process will the franchisor use to determine this?
- Whether the franchisee will be entitled to an exit payment at the end of the franchise agreement, and if so, how this will be determined.
- Whether the franchisee will have the right to sell the business at the end of the agreement. If so, whether the franchisor will have first right of refusal and how the market value will be determined.
- How capital expenditure during the term of the agreement will be taken into account at the end of the agreement.

CAPITAL EXPENDITURE REFORMS

Franchisors under the new Code will be prevented from requiring franchisees to undertake significant capital expenditure without notice or justification. However a franchisee may require the franchisee to undertake significant capital expenditure, unless one of the following exceptions apply:

- The expenditure is enclosed in the disclosure statement before entering or renewing or extending the term or scope of the agreement.
- The expenditure is to be incurred by all or most franchisees, and such expenditure is approved by the majority.
- The expenditure is because of legislative obligations.
- The expenditure is agreed to by the franchisee.
- If such expenditure is in the view of the franchisor to be necessary, it must be justified in a written statement given to each affected franchisee. It must show the rationale for the investment, the amount, the anticipated benefits and the expected risks associated with making the investment.

THE ROLE OF THE ACCC IN MANAGING THE CODE

- The role of the Australian Competition and Consumer Commission (ACCC), and the powers given to it under the new Code is to strengthen the local industry and to be a watchdog.
- It has already given warning to rogue franchise operators that its new powers give it the right to seek significant penalties for serious Code breaches.
- The ACCC has powers to issue infringement notices and seek penalties up to $51000 in court for serious breaches of certain Code provisions.
- In addition, the ACCC now also has powers to conduct random audits of franchisors to ensure that they comply with the law.
- Franchisors will now have to update their procedures to ensure that they comply with the Code and adhere to procedures as set out in the Code.

CHAPTER 31

INTERFERENCE BY THE LANDLORD IN THE RIGHTS OF THE RETAILER

Even if retailers have a lease which gives them the right to quiet enjoyment during the lease term, landlords always have the right to improve the value of their property. This may take the form of a landlord relocating the retailer to another tenancy in the centre, demolishing the retailer's premises or even closing a car park that supplies the retailer with a lot of traffic flow.

The State Acts allow the landlords to do this, but each action has consequences, and the landlord is expected to compensate the retailer. Let us now look at some of these interferences and how to negotiate them to your best advantage.

RELOCATION DURING THE LEASE TERM

- With the continuing upgrading and redevelopment of existing shopping centres, landlords will not hesitate to invoke their right under the lease to move you to a new location in the centre, but remember, that no retailer should allow themselves to be pushed around and should be prepared to invoke the protection given to them under the State Acts for such actions.
- Always try to have a relocation compensation clause for the fixtures and fittings that would be abandoned in the old store included in the lease. Some of the Acts now set out the amount of the compensation payable. These new compensation sections in the Acts therefore

become a deterrent to the landlord to" move you at will", solely to satisfy a tenancy mix requirement.

- Try to add a proviso in the lease so that the landlord will be responsible for all moving costs, including the costs of setting up temporary premises while your new location is being prepared.
- You should also request that a clause be added that makes provision for the waiving of your responsibility for the de-commissioning of your old store.

A MORE DETAILED LOOK AT COMPENSATION PROVISIONS IF A LANDLORD DISRUPTS A RETAIL BUSINESS

"ACQUAINTING YOURSELF WITH THIS INFORMATION CAN MEAN MONEY IN YOUR POCKET"

The lessor "is liable to pay" the lessee reasonable compensation for loss or damage suffered by the lessee if the lessor, or a person acting under the lessor's authority, acts in any of the following ways:

- He relocates the lessee's business to other premises during the term of the lease or any renewal of it.
- He substantially restricts the lessee's access to the leased shop.
- He takes any action (other than action under a lawful requirement), that substantially restricts or alters access by customers to the leased shop or the flow of customers to the retail shop.
- He causes significant disruption to the lessees trading in the leased shop.
- He does not take all reasonable steps to prevent or stop significant disruption within his control.
- He does not rectify as soon as possible any breakdown of plant or equipment under the lessor's care and maintenance, or any defect in the retail shopping centre or leased building containing the leased shop. (The exception is a defect that is due to a condition that would have been apparent to the lessee when he entered into the lease or when he/she accepted of assignment of the lease).
- He neglects to clean, maintain, or repaint the retail shopping centre

or leased building containing the leased shop or the part of the centre or building that under the lease is the lessor's responsibility.

- He causes the lessee to vacate the leased shop before the end of the lease or renewal due to the extension, refurbishment or demolition of the retail shopping centre or leased building containing the leased shop.
- **Section 43(2) of the Queensland Act further provides that:**
  "the lessor is liable to pay the lessee reasonable compensation for loss or damage suffered by the lessee because the lessee entered into the lease or a renewal of it, on the basis of a false and misleading statement or representation made by the lessor or any person acting under the lessor's authority or the leased shop was not available to the lessee for trading on the specified date in the disclosure statement because of the default of the lessor or anyone acting under the lessor's authority."

HOW THE AMOUNT OF COMPENSATION IS DECIDED

The amount of compensation payable in the previously mentioned situations will be decided by way of the dispute process. Any provision in a lease is void if the landlord tries to limit the amount of compensation payable under this section.

If the retailer believes that any of the above situations has occurred, he should immediately notify the lessor of his intentions to act under the Act. The amount of damages will be determined later.

Usually the amount to be claimed is" the gross profit that would have been earned on any fall of sales, compared to the same period in the previous year."

CHAPTER 32

LEASING PITFALLS IN UPSIZING YOUR EXISTING RETAIL STORE

LEASE IMPLICATIONS OF UPSIZING RETAIL PREMISES

To compete with large power stores, more and more speciality retailers are up sizing their premises. This often is achieved by either taking over the store next door when the lease on that store expires or by building onto the existing premises.

However, with the increasing number of sales on the internet following Covid-19, and the number of retailers implementing their own websites, it may be a time to reduce rather than upsize your premises.

LEASE NEGOTIATION CONSIDERATIONS

Any action to up-size could affect the lease on your existing store. Tenants who embark on this course of action should take the following into account: -

- When breaking down walls between two previously separate premises, always re-measure the total size of the premises. Often the new shop is not the sum of the two store sizes as stated in the individual leases and ends up being a different size.
- Rentals per square metre for larger stores are often lower than for speciality stores. Therefore, if you have upsized to a larger store, it is critical that you negotiate your rental for the combined premises

with the landlord. The new agreed rental should recognise the change in size. Do not simply add the rental paid on the new store to your existing store to arrive at the total rent payable.

- Ensure that the city council is aware of the consolidated status of the new store and you are assessed for rates and taxes accordingly.
- It is critical that the original lease is varied so that rental adjustments and termination of the lease on both stores are synchronised to a common date.
- Usually the upsizing of a store will entail the investment of a substantially increased amount of stock. This may also mean that you need a storeroom facility in the centre to carry reserve stock holdings.
- Try to negotiate acquiring a storeroom by way of a licence agreement to run simultaneously with the new lease and which starts and ends on the same dates.
- Usually storeroom facilities should be on a rental only basis with no outgoings payable on this area.
- Apart from the problems involved with renegotiating your lease, the retailer needs to fully assess the financial viability of an upsizing operation.

FINANCIAL CONSIDERATIONS AND COSTS

- Statistics show that doubling the size of the retail store will not necessarily result in a doubling of turnover.
- The larger area will require the retailer to keep a larger stock holding to adequately stock the new retail store.
- Unless arrangements can be made with suppliers to finance any additional stock holdings, substantial working capital will have to be provided by the retailer from their own financial resources.
- A larger retail store will more than likely require a complete new refit of the new premises with very little being salvaged from the existing retail store.
- Based on current costs, this could mean a large financial investment by the retailer and is likely to involve borrowing from a bank or financier.
- Fit-out costs will have to be amortised over the life of the lease and the projected profitability of the new" super" retail store will have to

be sufficient to absorb any reduction in equity and produce cash flow to repay the lender over the lease term.

- The servicing of a larger area requires an extra point of sale terminal as well as hiring staff to service any additional customers that will be drawn into the enlarged retail store.

- The retailer will not only have the cost of additional staff, but staff, will have to be available on Sundays and public holidays with the cost of penalty rates.

- A larger open style "super" retail store where customers select their goods and bring them to the cash registers makes the store more vulnerable to stealing. The retailer may either introduce additional security measures or be prepared to sustain a possible increase in stock shrinkage.

- When assessing the potential sales for a "super" retail store, it is important to remember that in a shopping centre, where you may have one or two other similar retailers as competitors, you may not be able to sell more of a particular line than you are currently selling simply because you have a larger area. This may mean that you may have to introduce additional lines and departments.

- Often new lines or departments carry a higher element of risk and unless you can find lines that will yield a higher gross profit than you are currently earning from the total retail store, these new departments can eat into your store profitability.

- Larger retailers have proved to be phenomenally successful in some major shopping centres, but often they have been established as "mini majors" from day one and not upsized from a smaller retail store.

- Possible deregulation of the pharmacy industry as proposed by the new Competition Review Report may well also act as a break on upsizing of pharmacy type retailing in the future.

However, if after consideration of all the facts you still wish to upsize, then I hope that at least you will now be cognisant of the possible pitfalls and dangers of this course of action.

CHAPTER 33

A LEASE FOR RETAIL PREMISES WHERE YOU OWN THE PROPERTY (FROM WHICH YOU RUN YOUR BUSINESS)

IMPROVE THE VALUE OF YOUR FAMILY ASSETS

The value of the property to a landlord is determined by the rent a retailer pays. The rent is then capitalized by a valuer at a percentage that is the yield an investor would be looking to receive from that property.

This yield ranges from 6% for a large shopping centre to 12% for smaller properties, depending on their location.

For Example:

In a property that a retailer owns and from which he trades has a capitalisation value of 10%, and he pays himself a notional $50,000 per annum in rent, the value of the property is:

$$\frac{\$50,000}{10\%}$$ (This is how property valuers and property owners would express this equation)

= $ 500,000

Against such a valuation a bank may be willing to advance the retailer 75% by way of a mortgage. He can therefore borrow 75% of $500,000 or $375,000 to acquire another property or invest it in his business.

He, then has an asset that he can underpin by entering a lease between himself and an entity owning the property, and thus have the ability to raise extra capital if he wishes.

If the business can afford it, he can then raise the rental further increasing the capital value of the business.

This is a good method of using the lease to improve the value of family assets.

CHAPTER 34

INITIATING AN EARLY LEASE NEGOTIATION WITH A LANDLORD

- Retailers are often faced with the dilemma as to when to start to negotiate a new lease with their landlord.
- Often the "gut" feeling is to leave the negotiation as close to the termination date of the lease as possible, in the hope that rentals will be lower at that stage. This may not turn out to be a good negotiation technique.
- If you begin discussions about 2 months before the end of the lease, you may find that the negotiations become protracted. You may start to panic about running out of lease time and accept terms and conditions in your lease which can later become onerous.
- For example, if you are contemplating the sale of your retail store and you have only two years to go with no further option, it is imperative that you initiate negotiations with your landlord for a new lease as soon as possible.
- The longer you leave it, the more difficult it will be to achieve your desired outcome. It is also exceedingly difficult to sell a retail store with a lease with only a short term to run on it.

THE IMPACT OF DECLINES IN RETAIL SALES ON NEGOTIATING TECHNIQES WITH LANDLORDS

From my observations, especially post Covid-19, the wave of publicity given to the problems experienced by small retailers on radio, television and in the press, has begun to have a positive effect on leasing negotiations with landlords. These include:

- The demand by landlords for a fixed annual increase of 5% per annum has now in several cases been watered down to CPI.
- More and larger fit out contributions are now being offered to retailers, particularly in new centers or in the redevelopment of existing centres.
- Relocation compensation formulas are now becoming standard in leases.
- More and more small retailers are achieving promotional rental rebates, thereby reducing rentals for up to twelve months until trading conditions in a shopping centre improve.
- Market reviews are often achieving much lower rentals in centres with known trading problems.
- Requests by retailers to introduce retailer favored clauses are becoming more easily accepted by landlords.
- But even more important for landlords, the basis used by many valuers to value property has now moved away from applying a cap rate to the current rental, but rather to the net present value of future rentals.
- Therefore, a long lease with the type of rentals paid by a retail store has additional importance to the landlord in the valuation of his property for the purposes of future bank borrowings.
- Opening negotiations with a landlord to initiate a new lease should not be a fearful exercise on the part of the retailer, but rather an opportunity to reset the level of occupancy cost for several years to come.

THE RIGHT TIME TO NEGOTIATE AN EARLY LEASE RENEWAL – FOR BOTH RETAILERS AND LANDLORDS

From my experience, the best times to open early negotiations include the following: -

For Retailers

- It will allow you the opportunity to initiate a new lease at *any time* during the lease term if you believe that it will give you an advantage. Then you will be able to take advantage of any falling rents, allow yourself to restore or extend the term of your lease, gain one further option period or even allow you the opportunity to bring your lease under the new retail tenancy legislation in your state.
- The strategy is to find an opportunity to initiate such an early lease renewal, which will give you an advantage but will also be beneficial to the landlord as well.
- If the lease calls for a market review where there is no "ratchet clause", in the lease that could result in a fall in rental for the landlord.

For Landlords

- On the change of retail tenancy legislation in your state, where the new act contains further rights for the landlord that are beneficial for him.
- If a centre is being redeveloped and the landlord wishes to relocate the retail store.
- On the termination of any exclusivity condition in your lease to allow further similar retailers to trade in the centre.

PART 2
LEASE NEGOTIATION

CHAPTER 35

RELIEF AGAINST FORFEITURE OF THE LEASE, WHERE A LANDLORD LOCKS OUT A RETAILER

This chapter applies mainly to Victorian retailers.

Whilst some states have some form of relief from forfeiture, if the landlord locks a tenant out, the state of Victoria has some special provisions of which the tenant should be aware. They are the following:

- In the event of a lockout from the retail premises, under section 89 of the Act, VCAT is the only body that can hear a claim by a retailer against a landlord for relief from forfeiture.
- Even though the landlord may have grounds for locking out the retailer, the retailer may seek relief from forfeiture via this section, providing he undertakes to fix the issue that caused the lockout.
- In addition, since section 92 provides that each party must pay its own costs, the landlord may not recover legal costs from the retailer. Thus, a landlord may win but loose.

This is an especially useful defence for a retailer who is being threatened with a lockout by the landlord. Therefore, the landlord or his agent should become familiar with the implication of this provision of the act.

CHAPTER 36

NEGOTIATING WITH YOUR LANDLORD DURING AN ECONOMIC DOWNTURN SUCH AS COVID-19

In the current economic climate, given falling retail sales, what avenues are open to the tenant to try to reduce overall occupancy costs given falling sales?

Retailers whose rents are up for renewal now are generally in the "box seat". Not many landlords are able to increase rents substantially on renewed leases, and some rents are even decreasing.

In the current climate, retailers should not be afraid to ask for a rental abatement.

NEGOTIATING TECHNIQUES

One of the most successful ways of getting a rebate is by writing a well-reasoned letter to the landlord setting out your position arising from the economic downturn and requesting a temporary rental rebate.

An example of such a typical letter requesting a rebate from a landlord could be on the following lines:

The Landlord

ABC Shopping Centre

Dear Sir

Re: Lease of XYZ Pty Ltd at the ABC Shopping Centre.

As you are no doubt aware. retail trading conditions in Australia have deteriorated substantially over the past few years especially during Covid-19, with most retailers experiencing lower sales and reduced margins. Our category of retail sales is no exception.

Our performance at the above centre has now reached a level at which we have no choice other than to seek some form of rental abatement from you. This abatement will hopefully assist us in the short term until retail conditions improve at the centre.

We are thus proposing the following for your consideration:

1. That we be provided with a rental abatement of $xxxx per month, either by way of a credit on our rental statement, or by way of an advertising concession. This abatement to be for a period of six months, when the continuation of the abatement can be reconsidered.
2. We will continue to pay our share of outgoings and marketing levy as per the lease.
3. Any rental increases due prior to the next six months will be waived and forgiven.

Looking forward to a favourable response to our request.

Yours Faithfully

OTHER USEFULL NEGOTIATION TECHNIQES

For those retailers who are about to renegotiate their leases the following leasing tips, will I hope ensure that you will be able to put into place a lease that will see you through the downturn and that will stand you in good stead over the next five years:

- Do not be afraid to ask for a substantial rental reduction at the start of the new lease. Landlords will be reluctant to lose tenants who pay their rent regularly.
- If your lease is due to expire in the next few months, ask for the first two years of the new lease term to be fixed at an agreed level with the first increase to be at the start of the third year.
- To overcome any landlord objections, insert a market review at the end of the third year of the lease. This will allow the rental to be restored to market rent if the economy has recovered by that time.
- Many retailers have a storage area within the retail store that is not used for displaying goods. Do not be afraid to split the area of the retail store in the new lease. For example, split the store into a 10m^2 a storeroom and a 140m^2 display area. The display area rent will be consistent with current rentals and the storage area will be consistent with current storage rates (e.g. $200 per square metre) with no outgoings payable for this storage area. This will reduce the overall rental cost for the two areas.
- Instead of entering into a new lease, ask for the current lease to be varied for a further two years at the same or reduced rental. As a result, you will avoid the necessity of a refurbishment of the store. You will also have a saving in working capital which is difficult to obtain in the current climate.
- Request that the landlord increase his contribution to the promotion fund to attract more traffic flow to the centre.
- Use the opportunity to vary your "permitted use" to include other usages for the retail store.
- Take the opportunity to again request for an option to be inserted in the lease that will assist with the resale of the retail store in the medium term.
- Request the landlord to provide you with a fit-out contribution to any fit out to the store that will be undertaken. This may be merely a cosmetic change to your store, but it will enhance it for a possible sale down the track.

PART 2
LEASE NEGOTIATION

CHAPTER 37

TYPES OF SHOPPING CENTRES

Leases are not the same and neither are shopping centres. The rent that you may have to pay for a similar store may differ vastly depending on the classification of each shopping centre.

The classification is dependent on the size of the centre, the major tenants, the annual turnover of all tenants and the traffic flow to that centre. If a shopping centre has a department store like Myers or David Jones, it has a higher ranking and commands a higher rental than if its major tenants consist of only discount department stores like Kmart, Target or Big W.

The number of supermarkets in a centre as its anchor tenants can also determine the rent paid under the lease.

In most publications dealing with shopping centres the following classifications are used:

- **Regional Centres:** These are major integrated retail centres under a single management, with at least one department store or discount department store of a minimum of 10000 square meters. The centre will have a total reporting gross lettable area (GLA) more than 25000 square meters. If it has three discount department stores (DDS) with a minimum of 5000 square meters in size and a GLA of 50000 square meters it can also be considered as a regional centre.
- **Top 10 Regional Centres:** These are the ten highest ranked regional centres based on total reported turnover.

- **Sub Regional Shopping Centres:** These usually consist of two major DDS and one or more supermarkets.

    Double DDS Centres: A type of sub regional centre with 2 DDS.

    Single DDS Centres: A type of sub regional centre with 1 DDS.
- **Supermarket Based Centres:** These are usually less than 10000 square metres and comprise of one or more major supermarkets along with a collection of food and non-food specialty shops and services in the same enclosed area.
- **Central Business District Centres (CBD Centres):** These are centres located in the central business district of Australian capital cities with either a national major or with a significant arcade.

CHAPTER 38

HOW TO ADMINISTER LEASES IN A PORTFOLIO

The setting up of an occupancy cost control document, is essential for the proper administration of a lease portfolio. If a retailer is sufficiently successful and has more than five stores maintaining of such a schedule is essential.

There are several helpful software packages on the market that offer this information. If you do not wish to go to this cost, you can set up a simple Excel spread sheet on your computer. If kept up to date, this will provide you with all the information that is required to monitor and administer occupancy costs.

The document should be linked to a separate spreadsheet that monitors the moving annual turnover of each store in your network. It sounds complicated but is easy to work with and delivers precise information and therefore is of great value.

What do we mean by moving annual turnover (MAT)?

This is a term often used in retail. It refers to the turnover of the store for the 12 months to the present date. Therefore, on 30 April 2021, the moving MAT becomes the 12 months to 30 April 2021. Once we know the May sales, we add this to the moving annual turnover figure and deduct the May of the previous year.

How to set up an Excel Spread Sheet

Three vertical line items are allocated to each store.

The following information is entered in each column about each store:

- **Store Location and store number**
- **Store Size:** xxx square metres
- **Base Rent:** $ Total Base Rent per lease

  $ Base Rent per square metre – by dividing the total base rent by the store size
- **Percentage Rent:** Calculated on an ongoing basis as per the formula in the lease
- **Total Rent:** Adding the base rent to the Percentage Rent
- **Rates and Taxes:** Rates and taxes on an annual basis. Some landlords charge monthly, others quarterly and, again, others annually.
- **Outgoings:** Enter total outgoings as per the landlord's estimate for the store.
- **Marketing Contribution:** Enter the total contribution as per the landlord's estimate for the store.
- **Total Occupancy Cost;** *Total* Dollar value calculated by adding total rent, rates and taxes, outgoings, and marketing contribution.

By expressing the total occupancy cost as a percentage of the moving annual turnover, we have "the occupancy cost to sales percentage for that store".

By dividing the total occupancy cost by the store size, we now have the total occupancy cost per square metre:

- **Sales MAT:** This is obtained by transferring the MAT from the attached spread sheet to this column for each store.
- **MAT per Square metre:** This is calculated by dividing the MAT by the store size.
- **Lease Commencement Date:** As per lease
- **Lease Expiry Date:** As per Lease
- **Lease Term and Options:** As per Lease
- **Date when Option Must be exercised:** As per lease
- **Details of last rent review:** As per lease.

However, if increase was waived or reduced by the landlord, this should be recorded in the schedule.

- **Date of next Review:** As per lease
- **Mode of next Review:** This is either be a sum fixed as per the lease, a percentage increase, CPI, or a market review. If the lease ends on the date of the next rent review, enter either "new lease" or "store closure".
- **Calculation of percentage rent:** This is usually a percentage of sales less base rent, or a percentage over and above a threshold figure.
- **Guarantee if and by whom:** As per lease
- **Special conditions in the lease:** As per lease.

Also include notations here like "lease incentive, for example, $20000 payable storeroom rent at $1000 per annum" or outgoings over base year 2021".

If we have the information available, we could add 3 additional columns, namely:

- **Centre traffic Flow:** As per information in Shopping Centre News etc.
- **Centre MAT:** As per information in Shopping Centre News etc.
- **Spend per Visitor to our Store:** Calculated by dividing your store MAT by centre traffic flow

CHAPTER 39

OPTION RENEWALS AND EXERCISING AN OPTION UNDER THE TERMS OF THE LEASE

Not many major landlords are prepared to offer tenants an option in their leases. However, smaller landlords who are trying to secure a good tenant for a long period, are prepared to offer options in leases.

If you have secured a lease with an option, there is a distinct process you need to go through to exercise such an option. The process is as follows:

- Your management schedule will alert you to the date by which you have to exercise your option.
- Remember that an option in a lease is a right that the tenant has and not the landlord.
- The tenant alone can decide whether he will exercise the option or not.
- Until you formally exercise the option, the landlord may be uncertain whether you will continue in occupation or whether he will have to find a new tenant, perhaps even at a reduced rental.
- Providing you ensure that you do not miss the deadline date, you could use the opportunity to improve your conditions in the lease by requesting the landlord to vary certain of the conditions in the lease as part of the option exercising process.
- Remember, that taking advantage of the landlord's vulnerability at this stage can often result in variations to clauses in the lease that are currently to the tenant's disadvantage.

- The ability of the tenant to take advantage of this situation will be decided by how the original option terms of the lease were negotiated.
- If you are able to negotiate options to renew the lease, make sure that they are not restrictive.
- Never accept a clause that grants an option "stating that the landlord could cancel this option if he wishes to redevelop or refurbish that part of the centre."
- To be on the safe side, you should always retain the right to exercise your option to take up premises in an alternate site in the centre. This applies particularly if there is to be a redevelopment of the centre involving your store.
- Avoid clauses in leases where the landlord demands "due and punctual performance" of all the terms and conditions of the lease throughout the term as a pre-condition to the exercise of an option.
- Be sure to have your solicitor water down such a clause as outlined previously, to enable you to exercise the option provided you are not in breach of the lease" at the time of the notice" exercising the option, or at the expiration of the term of the lease. This does not apply to some minor breach during the term of the lease which you may have already rectified.

LETTERS TO THE LANDLORD EXERCISING THE OPTION

If you do exercise the option for a further term, the retailer *must under no circumstances* write a conditional exercise of the option.

An example of letter you do not write

"In terms of clause 4 of the lease, we hereby exercise our option for a further term of 3 years providing we can arrive at a lower rental than at present".

This is a conditional exercise of the option and if the landlord so desires, he may argue that you have not exercised your option.

This is an example of the letter that you do write:

In terms of clause 4 of the lease, we hereby exercise our option for a further term of 3 years.

Then a day or so later you may write the following letter to the landlord.

As you are aware, we have exercised our option for a further term of 3 years. However, we are unhappy with our present rental and before we proceed to market value as per the lease, we would like to meet with you to discuss a possible lower rental.

PART 2
LEASE NEGOTIATION

CHAPTER 40

WHAT CONSTITUTES RETAIL PREMISES SO THAT THEY FALL UNDER THE PROTECTION OF THE RETAIL LEASES ACT IN VICTORIA?

In all states other than Victoria, the premises that fall under the Act are usually listed as a schedule to the Act in that state. However, this is not the case in Victoria.

In Victoria, the section of the Act dealing with retail premises is complicated, due mainly to the wording of the Retail Leases Act. Therefore, much interpretation is involved. Each lease must be assessed individually. As this is a complex area, a consulting specialist in the field is often your best course of action.

The Small Business Commissioner in Victoria issued the following guidelines on what constitutes retail premises in Victoria.

THE STATEMENT VERBATIM

I have set out the following guidelines in full for the benefit of retailers and other businesses that may offer goods or services for sale, for example legal and accounting firms. The statement must be read in conjunction with section 4 of the Acts. Retailers and other providers of goods and services should read the statement carefully before entering a lease in Victoria.

The criteria for determining whether the premises are "retail premises" are set out in section 4 of the Act. The premises will be "retail premises" if the premises, or part of the premises, under the terms of the lease, are used are to be used wholly or predominately for the sale or hire of goods by retail or the retail provision of services (section 4(1) (a)).

Further, section 4(1) (b) provides that the Minister may determine that a specified business or specified kind of business is "retail" for the purposes of section 4.

Note, the word "lease" which is used in section 4(1) is defined in section 3 of the Act as meaning a lease, sub lease, agreement for lease or sub lease whether or not in writing.

Guiding principles to determine "retail premises"

The Act does not define "retail". Therefore, an interpretation of the term must rely on its ordinary meaning. Therefore in order to determine whether the premises are "retail" each lease must be assessed individually, having regard to the nature and provisions of the lease, including the actual or intended use of the premises under the terms of the lease, and the actual circumstances in this respect.

The following guidelines derived from leading decisions of the Tribunal and courts are provided to assist in assessing whether the premises are "retail" premises". Express or implied prohibition on retail use.

If the lease expressly or impliedly prohibits retail use of the premises, there is an assumption that the premises are not retail. An example of an implied covenant prohibiting retail use of the premises is a covenant requiring the tenant to comply with planning requirements and lawful use of the premises. For example, the local law and/or planning laws may prohibit the premises from being used as retail - that is, the premises may be located in an "industrial" zone.

How the premises are "used, or are to be used"

In the absence of an express or implied prohibition, the way the premises are used, or are to be used, under the terms of the lease must be considered.

Actual usage may, in some circumstances, assist in the interpretation of the terms of the lease in this respect, but cannot contradict them. From the language of section 11(2) of the Act, the way the premises are used or are to be used is assessed at the time the lease is entered. For some leases, there may be no actual use at the time the lease is entered.

For example, when an agreement for a lease is signed for the purpose of erecting a building on the premises, the commencement date of the lease is the date the works are completed and the premises are ready for trade. In these situations, the use is assessed according to the express or implied terms of the lease (this may be found in the "permitted use" clause).

However if it is unclear from the permitted use clause whether a retail use is permitted, and the landlord and tenant are in dispute as to whether the premises are to be used for retail purposes of a particular kind or kinds, the Tribunal or a court (as the case may be) is likely to explore what the intentions of the landlord and tenant were when they entered into the lease to the extent that this intention can be determined objectively, that is, that the parties cannot give evidence as to their subjective intention.

Sale to the "ultimate consumer"

The provision of goods or services generally involves a sale to an "ultimate consumer". This is the ordinary meaning of "retail" consistent with definitions found in various authoritative dictionaries. These dictionary definitions indicate that it is implicit in the concept of "sale" that goods are sold at a price, which involves the payment of money. The position is similar with respect to the meaning of "hire" (i.e. "hire" does not mean merely "lend", gratuitously, as "sale" does not involve "giving" in the usual sense).

The ultimate consumer is generally a member of the public; however the ultimate consumer can also be a class of persons. For example, a retail shop selling books and information products that are only sold to members of a certain professional association would still involve a sale to the "ultimate consumer".

In respect of the kind of sales made to the ultimate consumer, many, if not most are for household or personal use. However the meaning of "retail" is not limited to these situations and may include large commercial transactions, providing they are made to the "ultimate consumer".

It should not be overlooked that the definition of "retail" in the Act also includes the hire of goods and, additionally, includes the retail provision of services and therefore the "ultimate consumer" test is also to be applied to these classes of retail, as indicated by previous Tribunal and court decisions.

These decisions do, however, indicate that the retail provision of services may take place in circumstances where, for example, professional services are provided for an intermediary where the "ultimate consumer" pays for those professional services and the nature and content of the "product" of those services is not changed in any substantial way by the intermediary. An example is the professional advice of a patent attorney which is provided to a firm of solicitors on behalf of their client where the advice of the patent attorney is passed on to the solicitors' client.

Sales in small quantities may be retail

If the premises are used for the sale of goods in small quantities to the "ultimate consumer", this may be indicative of the sale being "retail". However, the quantity of goods sold is not necessarily a decisive factor.

Retail excludes wholesale

The concept of "retail" excludes sales by wholesale. Wholesale sales are the converse to sales to the "ultimate consumer" discussed above, as commonly wholesale sales are to retailers, industrial, institutional and commercial users. These recipients acquire the goods for the purpose of resale to others who will be the ultimate consumer, of a retail sale.

Also, premises where wholesale sales are carried out, such as factories or warehouses, are generally not premises where the public are invited, and are not places where retail sales are expected to be made to the ultimate consumer. Note however that factory outlets, or second's shops, in factories or warehouses are likely to be exceptions as they involve retail sales.

Example:

A hardware shop selling nuts and bolts to the general public would be "retail premises", whereas a warehouse selling nuts and bolts to hardware shops would not.

Similarly, an industrial premise where nuts and bolts are manufactured, and sold to distributors, who then sell their products to wholesalers, would not be "retail".

Occupancy costs? – The $1million dollar rule

If the lease exceeds $1miion dollars in rental it may be excluded from the provisions of the Act.

The term "occupancy costs" is defined in section 4(3) as being the total of:

- *the rent (excluding turnover rent);*
- *outgoings of a prescribed kind; and*
- *other costs of a prescribed kind*

payable under the lease. Outgoings of a prescribed kind and other costs are set out in regulation 7 of the Regulations (see paragraph 9.4 below).

Lease incentives included as "rent"?

Rent reductions, abatements, or other lease incentives provided for under a separate deed to the lease may not be considered effective to reduce the amount of rent payable under the lease for the purpose of calculating "occupancy costs" as the deed may be considered an anti-avoidance mechanism, and runs the risk of being made void if disputed under sections 94(2) and (3) of the Act.

What are "prescribed" outgoings and costs?

Regulation 7 of the Retail Leases Regulations 2003 prescribes the kind of outgoings and other costs for the purposes of sections 4(3) (b) and (c). The prescribed outgoings are as follows:

- *amenity facilities, including gardening and landscaping, public address and music systems.*
- *building or retail shopping centre management services, including temperature control, insurance, pest control and ventilation.*
- *communication facilities, including telephones and post boxes;*
- *customer facilities, including car parking, lifts, escalators, and child minding.*

PART 2
LEASE NEGOTIATION

- *hygiene services, including cleaning, garbage collection and disposal, sewerage and waste disposal.*
- *information services, including customer traffic flow and other building intelligence information, information directories and signage.*
- *rates, taxes, levies, premiums, charges and fees, including municipal council rates and charges, sewerage and drainage rates and charges, administration costs, audit fees and management fees;*
- *repairs and maintenance services.*
- *security services, including emergency systems and fire protection equipment; and*
- *utility services, including electricity, gas, oil, water and energy management systems.*

The prescribed other costs are as follows:

Advertising and promotional services, including marketing fund contributions. These outgoings and costs have been prescribed for the purpose only to calculate the "occupancy costs". Therefore, outgoings which fall outside of these categories will not be included in the calculation of "occupancy costs"; however they can be recovered from the tenant, provided they do not otherwise offend the Act.

This means that there may be leases that have a total liability for costs in excess of $1,000,000 per annum which still come within the application of the Act. That is, the total liability for costs is made up of a component of prescribed occupancy costs which is less than $1,000,000, and a component of other non-prescribed costs which, in addition to the total of prescribed occupancy costs, exceeds $1,000,000.

Time occupancy cost is calculated.

It appears from section 11(2) of the Act that the total occupancy cost is to be calculated at the time the lease is entered into. However, when leases are entered into, some of the actual costs are unknown. Actual costs may become known only at a later point during the first term of the lease. The question this raises is whether the total occupancy cost should be calculated on the actual costs, or the estimated costs.

In cases where the occupancy cost borders on the $1,000,000 threshold, it would be unreasonable for the parties to wait until all actual costs are ascertained before it is known whether the lease is subject to the Act or not. This would also create a burdensome administrative task of refunding or back charging the fees that are prohibited from being recovered under the Act.

In the circumstances, it appears that practical necessity dictates that an estimate of costs at the commencement will be sufficient. Of course, the estimated costs should be reasonable, and where ascertainable, have regard to last year's actual costs.

The commercial premises exception

Leases of commercial premises take many forms, for example, professional suites, head administration offices, and call centres. Some commercial premises will fall into the definition of "retail" by virtue of the way the premises are used, as opposed to the lease's permitted use, which is often termed "office".

On the other hand, some leases will involve a use of the premises merely for office purposes where no retailing is involved. These may include leases of premises to management or administration companies that provide a service to a retailer or other intermediary (as opposed to the ultimate consumer). Therefore for example, the "head office" premises to a fashion retailer or the office of the master franchisor may not be retail.

However this may differ where the office is an essential component of the retail business, particularly where customer orders or enquiries are handled from that office. In this instance, the office may be considered "retail".

The Minister's Determination

A lease of premises where the retail provision of services occurs would, in the first instance, be a "retail premises" to the extent that the criteria in section 4(1)(a) are satisfied. However, the Minister has made a Determination limiting the application of the Act to these "commercial leases".

The Determination made for the purposes of section 4(2) (f) and published in the Victorian Government Gazette No. s 75 (30 April 2003) provides as follows:

PART 2
LEASE NEGOTIATION

PREMISES NOT CONSTITUTING RETAIL PREMISES

This determination is made under Section 5(1) (c) of the Retail Leases Act 2003. This determination does not apply to:

- *premises that under the terms of the lease relating to the premises or part are used, or are to be used, wholly or predominantly for the sale or hire of goods by retail;*
- *retail premises located in a retail shopping centre.*

Acting under Section 5 (1) (c) of the Retail Leases Act 2003, I determine that the following kind of premises are premises to which Section 4(2) (f) applies:

Premises that are located entirely within a building which, under the terms of the lease relating to the premises, or part of the premises, are used, or are to be used, wholly or predominantly for the retail provision of services, other than premises located entirely on any one or more of the first three storeys in a building, excluding any basement levels.

This determination comes into effect on 1 May 2003.

This Determination excludes premises or part of the premises in a building that are used wholly or predominately for the retail provision of services, other than those located on any one of the first three storeys of the building. In calculating the first three storeys of the building, the basement levels are not included.

The Determination does not affect the application of the Act to any premises in the building which are used wholly or predominately for the retail sale of goods. The Determination also does not affect any premises in a retail shopping centre which are used wholly or predominately for the retail provision of services (and for the retail provision of goods for that matter). These types of premises are still "retail premises" within the meaning of the Act, providing that the criteria in section 4(1) are otherwise.

PRACTICAL TIPS FOR CALCULATING STORIES

The third storey of the building may not necessarily be the third floor of the building. That is, if there is a "ground floor", this would be counted as the first storey. Similarly, what is called the "basement" level in the building's directory or elevator may not be a basement in the ordinary sense of the word. "Basement" is ordinarily taken to mean the car park level or the storage level, which is usually uninhabitable. But in some office buildings, the "basement level" is occupied by tenants, commonly by food court tenants, travel and real estate agents, beauty salons, newsagencies, etc. So how are the storeys to be calculated? intended that the use of the term "excluding any basement levels" is for the purpose only of calculating the three stories. It is irrelevant that there may be retail premises located on a "basement" level. Retail premises located on the basement levels will still come within the Act. Therefore, to assist in determining the first storey (which then allows the calculation of the remaining 2 stories) the first floor above the storey which is categorised as "basement" should be established. In most cases, this will be the "ground" floor, or if there is no ground floor, the "first" floor. A simple way to determine this is to have regard to the way the stories are described in the building's tenant directory or elevator.

Some examples:

- The directory describes a medical suite as being located on "Floor 3". The floors of the building are "Basement", "Floor 1", "Floor 2", and "Floor 3". In this example, the relevant three stories of the building, excluding the basement levels, are ""Floor 1", "Floor 2", and "Floor 3". As the medical suite is located within the first three stories of the building, the Act will apply to the medical suite premises and any other retail premises in the building.
- The directory describes a hairdresser as being located on the "Basement". The floors of the building are "Basement", "Floor 1", "Floor 2", and "Floor 3". In this example, the hairdresser is located on a basement level. Accordingly, it is not necessary to determine the relevant three stories of the building. The Act will apply to the hairdresser's premises and any other retail premises in the building.
- The directory describes an accountant's practice as being located on "Floor 2". The floors of the building are "Basement 2", "Basement 1", "Ground 1", "Ground 2", "Floor 1", and "Floor 2". In this example, the relevant three stories of the building, excluding the basement levels, are "Ground 1", "Ground 2", and "Floor 1". As the accountant's practice

is located above the first three stories of the building, the Act will not apply to the accountant's premises

- The directory describes the car park (which involves a paying service) as being located on "Basement 1 – 3". The floors of the building are "Basement 3", "Basement 2", "Basement 1", "Ground", "Floor 1", and "Floor 2". In this example, the car park is located on the basement levels. Accordingly, it is not necessary to determine the relevant three stories of the building. The Act will apply to the car park premises and any other retail premises in the building.
- The directory describes an architect's firm as being located on the "Mezzanine". The floors of the building are "Basement", "Ground", "Mezzanine" and "Floor 1". In this example, the relevant three storeys of the building, excluding the basement levels, are "Ground", "Mezzanine" and "Floor 1". As the architect's firm is located within the first three storeys of the building, the Act will apply to the architect's premises.
- The directory describes a law practice as being located on "Floors 2 and 3". The floors of the building are "Basement", "Ground", "Floor 1", "Floor 2", "Floor 3" and "Floors 4-10". In this example, the relevant three storeys of the building, excluding the basement, are "Ground", "Floor 1" and "Floor 2". As the law practice is not located entirely on one or more of the first three storeys of the building, the Act will not apply to the law practice.

It is clear that each building must be considered in isolation, and a common sense approach employed in each instance.

Definition of "retail premises" – changes from the previous Acts

Franchises

Provided that the contractual arrangement that the franchisee holds with the franchisor is a lease or sublease, and all the criteria in section 4(1) are satisfied (see paragraph 6, above) and none of the exemptions in section 4(2) apply (see paragraph 8, above), the premises will be "retail premises". This contrasts with the 1986 Act and the 1998 Act which excluded franchisees from the application of those Acts if the tenant operated under a name or mark identifying, commonly associated with or controlled by the landlord.

Carrying on a business

It is not a requirement for the application of the Retail Leases Act 2003 that the tenant is carrying on a "business" of retailing in order for the premises to be considered "retail" pursuant to section 4(1) of the Act. The only requirement under the Act in this respect is that the tenant is permitted to use the premises for retailing "under the terms of the lease" (see section 4(1)). This is in contrast to the 1986 Act and the 1998 Act which required the tenant to be "carrying on of a business involving" retailing. Therefore tenants who operate not-for-profit organisations (for example, op-shops) are now clearly included in the application of the Act.

Part of" premises

The definition of "retail premises" in the Act now contains the additional words "or a part of premises" which seemingly widens the scope of premises included in the application of the Act.

Although it is not free from doubt, it would appear that the effect of the addition of these words was intended to be limited to accommodating mixed retail and residential use of premises as contemplated by section 95 of the Act (which makes provision for maintenance in good repair of the residential area where the Residential Tenancies Act 1997 does not apply). An interpretation of these provisions which applied the "wholly or predominantly" test in section 4(1) with respect to part only of the premises would produce a far broader application of the Act – beyond what would generally be regarded as retail premises – than Parliament would be likely to have intended. For example, this interpretation of the Act would capture leases where the premises are used almost exclusively for wholesale, industrial, manufacturing or office uses but which also contain a small retail outlet occupying a very small part of the premises where sales to the public are undertaken.

In borderline cases, it may be unclear whether the premises are used wholly or predominately for wholesale, manufacturing, industrial (etc.) purposes or whether the premises are used wholly or predominately for the retail sale of goods. Consider for example, a dairy manufacturing premise that contains a manufacturing part and a retail sales part, both of equal area. In this case, it is unclear what the premises are used wholly or predominately for. It would therefore be advisable to at least treat the retail part as a "retail premises". This can be done by drawing up two leases, one for the "retail premises" and the other for the manufacturing area. In the alternative, one "retail premises" lease can be drawn up that covers the whole of the premises - this will be easier to administer than having two leases for the premises.

When "retail premises" determined

As discussed above, section 11(2) of the Retail Leases Act 2003, in effect, provides that the time for determining whether the premises are "retail" is at the time the lease is entered into or renewed (see sections 7 and 9 for definition of "entered into" and "renewed" respectively). This contrasts with the 1986 Act and the 1998 Act which did not contain such a provision. Under these Acts, the applicability of the Act could be affected throughout the term of the lease and therefore could cease to apply or begin to apply at any time during the lease term.

Because of the effect of section 11(2), if the Act applies to the lease when entered into or renewed, and subsequently there is a change in circumstances during the term of the lease that affects the applicability of the Act, the lease will remain subject to the Act. Similarly, where the Act does not apply when the lease is entered, the lease will not become subject to the Act if there is a change in circumstances affecting its applicability. Therefore, the status of the applicability of the Act is determined at the outset and does not change during the term of the lease. Examples of the circumstances that may change include an increase (or decrease) in the total occupancy cost, or the tenant becoming (or ceasing to be) a listed company.

As such, the only opportunity for the status of the applicability of the Act to change is upon renewal of the lease. For example, a lease is entered into with a public company tenant for five years with a five-year option for renewal. At the time the lease was entered into, the Act did not apply. In year 3, the lease is assigned to a non-public company. There is no variation to the terms of the lease and therefore the assignment does not amount to a new lease (section 8 of the Act). For the remaining two years of the initial term, the Act will not apply. However, upon the lease renewal (because the renewal of a lease is regarded as the granting of a new lease), the applicability of the Act changes and the Act may then apply to the lease for the five year option term. The same would apply if the lease term were extended by agreement. This results in a surrender and termination of the existing lease and the grant of a new lease for the remainder of the then extended term.

Thus it is essential when entering into a lease for a tenancy in a CBD building selling goods and services and you want the protection of the Retail Tenancy Act that you pick one of the first 3 floors of that building.

CHAPTER 41

WHO IS RESPONSIBLE FOR PAYING FOR THE LEGAL COSTS IN PREPARING A LEASE, AND THE STAMP DUTY ON A LEASE?

The law relating to who is responsible for paying the legal costs of preparing a lease, and the stamp duty on a lease payable to the state government, varies from state to state. This could be a substantial cost to a new retailer as he may have to pay his own legal costs as well as the legal costs of the landlord. These costs need to be considered in your decision to enter the lease.

New South Wales

A tenant is not liable to pay for lease preparation costs except any amendments to the lease that are requested or negotiated.

It is worth noting, that a tenant cannot be compelled to use a lawyer nominated by the landlord.

No stamp duty is payable on leases.

Victoria

The landlord cannot charge the tenant for legal costs and other expenses relating to the negotiation, preparation, and execution of the lease nor for the costs of obtaining the mortgagees consent nor the landlord's requirement to comply with the Act.

This does not preclude the landlord recovering the legal costs in respect of an assignment of the lease, including the investigation of the proposed assignee.

No stamp duty is payable on leases.

Queensland

The landlord cannot charge the tenant the legal costs for preparing, renewing, or extending a lease.

The landlord can however charge the tenant for the registration of the lease, survey fees associated with the registration of the lease, obtaining the mortgagees consent, the costs of any actual variation to an ongoing lease, and the landlord's consent to a sublease or licence.

No stamp duty is payable on leases.

Australian Capital Territory

Each party must bear its own legal costs. However, if the tenant wishes to have the lease registered under the Land Titles Act, he must pay for registration costs of the lease and the costs of obtaining the mortgagee's consent.

It is worth noting, that a tenant cannot be compelled to use the lawyer nominated by the landlord.

No stamp duty is payable in the ACT.

I would recommend that all leases be registered if you are opening a store in the ACT.

Northern Territory

A tenant is liable for only reasonable legal expenses incurred by the landlord. He must however, be provided with an account showing how the amount has been calculated. This must also be shown in the disclosure statement.

A landlord can recover legal costs from the tenant where the prospective tenant enters into negotiations and then withdraws.

It is also worth noting that a tenant cannot be compelled to use the lawyer nominated by the landlord.

Stamp duty is not payable.

South Australia

The tenant is required to pay one half of the landlord's legal costs unless he withdraws from the negotiations. If the retailer withdraws, he may be required to pay the full amount.

The tenant is expected to pay mortgagees consent fees.

The tenant is not required to pay anything unless he receives a detailed account of how the charges are made up.

No stamp duty is payable.

West Australia

The Act is silent on this issue and therefore will have to be negotiated between the parties. I would recommend that each party pays its own legal fees.

No stamp duty is payable.

Tasmania

A tenant is not liable to pay for lease preparation costs except where any amendments to the lease that are requested or negotiated.

A landlord can still recover legal costs from the tenant where the prospective tenant enters negotiations and then withdraws.

Mortgagees fees are payable.

It is also worth noting, that a tenant cannot be compelled to use the lawyer nominated by the landlord.

No stamp duty is payable.

CHAPTER 42

CONCLUSION - CHECKLIST OF TENANT'S RIGHTS UNDER THE RETAIL LEASES ACTS

As indicated in earlier chapters, the Retail Tenancy Acts in the various states and territories give the tenant rights and protection from landlords. They also stop landlords from requesting certain clauses in leases which are unreasonable. The Acts also aim to create a level playing field during the negotiation process.

Whilst this chapter is not meant to be a legal lesson, and you will need to consult a lawyer in most cases, it is crucial for tenants to have this information available when negotiating a lease with a landlord. Though some points may have been included earlier, they are worth repeating. The checklist is again broken up by state as the law is different in each state. We will be looking at the three major states of Victoria, New South Wales, and Queensland.

VICTORIA

- There is no specific list of premises attached to the Victorian Act as indicated previously. However, you are considered to be retailer and fall under the act, if you use the premises predominantly for the sale or hire of retail goods or services, the lease is for more than one year, you are not a subsidiary of a public company listed on a world stock exchange and the total occupancy cost does not exceed $1m.
- The landlord is responsible for the repair of the premises, provided

that damage has not been caused by negligence of the tenant. The landlord may not recover the cost of this repair through the outgoings schedule.

- The landlord has an obligation to make statistical information about the performance of a centre available to the tenant.
- A copy of the proposed lease and a copy of the information brochure must be given to the tenant before any negotiations commence. A disclosure statement and a copy of the final lease are required at least 7 days before the lease is entered into. If you do not receive a disclosure statement, the tenant after giving notice to the landlord may withhold rent.
- If the premises are not available for handover on the date specified in the disclosure statement, the tenant is not liable to pay rent.
- The landlord must give a copy of the signed lease back to the tenant within 28 days after receiving a copy of the lease from the tenant.
- If the lease is to be for less than 5 years, the tenant must request the Small Business Commissioner to certify a shorter term.
- A tenant in a shopping centre is not responsible to pay for outgoings relating to capital costs, depreciation, sinking funds for capital works, interest on landlord's borrowings, rent under a head lease, rent for other properties and land tax.
- The tenant is not expected to provide his turnover figures unless the lease contains a percentage rent clause.
- Goods and Services Tax must be deducted from sales provided by a landlord to a tenant in respect of percentage rent sales.
- A provision in a lease is void if it prevents the rent falling in the case of a market review of rent.
- A tenant is not required to pay "key money" for entering into a lease.
- If the lease contains an option, the landlord must notify the tenant of the date after which the option is no longer exercisable, at least 6 months and not more than 12 months before that date.
- If the landlord does not give the notice required, the option remains exercisable until 6 months after the landlord gives the required notice. The lease will then continue under the "holding over provisions" of the lease.
- A clause in a lease is void if it prevents the tenant from joining a tenant's association.

- The Shop Trading Reform Act makes lease provisions void if they require the trade on Sundays. Remember, undue influence or pressure from the landlord, to trade on Sundays may amount to unconscionable conduct.
- Any party to a lease can initiate a dispute. All retail tenancy disputes are initially handled by the Small Business Commissioner's office by way of mediation. Costs of mediation are shared in proportions agreed to by the parties, or if they cannot agree, equally. If mediation as certified by the Commissioner has failed, then it may be referred to the Victorian Civil and Administration Tribunal (VCAT).
- Tenants cannot be held liable to indemnify landlords beyond the liability they would have had in Common Law.
- If the tenant is required to pay a security bond, it must be held in a separate account and the landlord must notify the tenant about all interest earned. The bond forms part of the overall security for the tenancy, which is refundable at the end of the lease.
- The landlord cannot reasonably refuse a bank guarantee in place of a security deposit.
- A provision in a lease requiring the tenant to undertake any promotion or advertising of the tenants business is regarded as void. However, the tenant may still be required to pay an amount into a marketing fund together with other tenants in order to promote the centre. The tenant is entitled to receive from the landlord a marketing plan one month before the start of each accounting year. In the case of an opening promotion contribution, details of the proposed expenditure must be made available to the tenant, one month before the promotion.
- Neither a landlord nor a tenant can engage in unconscionable conduct. The Act sets out a list of examples of what is considered unconscionable conduct. However, under the Act, it is not considered unconscionable conduct, if the landlord institutes a dispute, fails to enter into a lease or renew a lease, does not agree to have an independent valuation of a current market review. Remember that a tenant has 6 years to issue a claim with VCAT for loss or damage sustained by a landlord for unconscionable conduct.
- If the leased premises or the building in which they are located are damaged, the tenant does not have to pay rent or outgoings. If repairs

to the building are impracticable, the tenant or the landlord may terminate the lease.

- If the landlord has to carry out works in the building that affects the tenants business, 60 days' notice in writing to the tenant is required. If the premises have to be demolished, the Act in section 56 sets out a detailed formula as to how the tenant is to be compensated,

- If the tenant is to be relocated to a new tenancy, again the Act sets out the conditions under which such relocation is to take place.

- A lease cannot be terminated simply because the tenant has not achieved a certain level of sales.

- The Act has a ban on a restriction of trade if a tenant also trades in premises outside the centre.

- A lease provision is void if it limits the tenant's rights to engage persons doing work on the premises other than under the specified limits of competence and complying with any award affecting the shopping centre.

- A provision in a lease is void if it requires the premises to be refurbished, unless it indicates the nature, extent and timing of the refurbishment or refitting.

- If the lease contains a right for the tenant to use part of the premises as a residential area and the Residential Tenancies Act does not apply to the lease, the landlord must ensure that the residential area is maintained in good repair.

- The new Act requires a landlord to return a tenant's security deposit within 30 days of the lease ending, provided that the tenant has performed all of the obligations under the lease. Previously, the act provided that deposits must be returned "as soon as practicable". This applied from 1 October 2020.

- A new section in the Act, enables a tenant to request an early rent review if the tenant has an option to renew in its lease. To trigger the review, the tenant must give the landlord notice within 28 days of receiving the landlord's renewal notice. After Covid19 tenants with options in their lease should consider this option on the impact on their lease in the option period. Examine the full impact of the new section 28 if you are considering this.

- A new section 28 of the Act, also provides that if a tenant has exercised its option to renew but has not requested an early review, to give the landlord written notice in the cooling-off period (14 days after the option is exercised), that the tenant no longer wishes to renew the lease, then the lease will be extended by 14 days, the lease and is taken not to have been renewed. The tenant is also not able to exercise an option to renew the lease.

NEW SOUTH WALES

- If the store is over 1000m2 in size, it does not fall under the Act. However, public companies under this size do fall under the Act.
- Leases for under 6 months in duration do not fall under the Act. The use of the technique of retaining a tenant whilst the centre is under construction must be watched by a retailer. It gives the tenant no protection for compensation during this construction phase. If you have to take out this type of lease, insist that it be for 6 months and 1day.
- Premises that form part of the office tower of a shopping centre do not fall under the Act.
- There is no obligation to pay rent and for the tenant to take possession of the premises, unless the landlord has completed the fit out.
- Unlike the situation in Victoria, the creation of a sinking fund for future repairs and maintenance, is permitted in New South Wales.
- Land Tax is permitted to be charged to tenants in this state. However, this is based on a single ownership basis which is more favourable to a tenant. At the time of writing there have been moves to stop land tax being charged to tenants under the Act in that state.
- If there is a market review in a lease, this must be completed 3 to 6 months prior to the date any option is to be exercised.
- In the case of promotion and advertising charges for a centre made to the tenant by the landlord, the landlord must provide a marketing plan, a list of expenditure and an account for any unspent contributions.
- A copy of the lease and a retail tenancy guide, must be provided to the tenant when negotiations commence otherwise a fine is imposed on the landlord. If the tenant does not receive a disclosure statement at least 7 days before the lease is entered into a fine is imposed. The same applies to a renewal.
- The tenant is not liable for fit out costs, services, equipment,

refurbishment or refitting if these are not disclosed in the disclosure statement.

- A lease can be terminated by the tenant within 6 months of the lease being entered into, if the landlord fails to provide a disclosure statement, or if the statement is incomplete, materially false or misleading.

- A copy of the lease is to be given to the tenant within 1 month of registration of the lease, subject to the time it takes to obtain mortgagees or head lessor's consent.

- The tenant has no liability to pay for any fit-out costs or equipment, refurbishment or refitting, if they are not disclosed in the disclosure statement. The tenant is not liable to pay for fit out works that are more than the agreed maximum amount.

- A provision in a lease, requiring the tenant to undertake any promotion or advertising of the tenant's business are regarded as void. However, the tenant may still be required to pay an amount into a marketing fund together with other tenants to promote the centre.

- The landlord must provide the tenant with a statement every 6 months concerning expenditure from any promotion or advertising fund. If this is not provided, the tenant can withhold any contributions to the fund until it is received. Any unspent money must be carried forward to future expenditure.

- A lease cannot be terminated simply because the tenant has not achieved a certain level of sales.

- The Act also has a ban on a restriction on trade if a tenant also trades in premises outside the centre.

- Rental increases of CPI plus a percentage are allowed in New South Wales but not in Victoria.

- A provision in a lease which prevents the rent falling on a market review is regarded as void.

- If the parties cannot agree on the market rent, then the Act allows the retailer to apply to the Tribunal to set the market rent.

- If the tenant must be relocated in a shopping centre, he is entitled to payment by the landlord of the reasonable costs of relocation.

- A landlord can withhold his consent for the assignment of the lease if the assignee proposes to change the usage or the assignee has financial and retail skills inferior to the assignor or has not complied with the lease.

- Key money cannot be requested for consent.
- Goods and Services Tax must be deducted from sales provided by the landlord to the tenant in respect of percentage rent sales.
- A guarantor is no longer liable on the lease, if the person assigning the lease for an ongoing business, has handed over a copy of the disclosure statement to the assignee.
- A clause in a lease is regarded as void if it prevents the tenant from joining a tenant's association.
- If the tenant is required to pay a security bond, it must be lodged with the Rental Bond Board within 20 days after receipt of the bond. Both the landlord and tenant must sign any application to pay out money from this account.
- The landlord cannot reasonably refuse a bank guarantee in place of a security deposit.
- If the leased premises or the building in which the retailer is located is damaged, the tenant does not have to pay rent or outgoings. If repairs are impracticable to the building, the tenant or the landlord may then terminate the lease.
- If the landlord must carry out works in the building that affects the tenant's business, 90 days' notice in writing to the tenant is required. Section 34, sets out the formula for compensation to be paid. If the premises must be demolished, the Act in section 35 sets out a detailed formula as to how the tenant is to be compensated. It is wise to familiarise yourself with these provisions.
- A lease provision is void if it limits the tenant's rights to engage persons to do work on the premises, other than specifying limits of competence and complying with any award affecting the shopping centre.
- A refurbishment requirement is void unless it sets out in general terms, the nature, extent, and timing of the refurbishment.
- Where the tenancy is part of a strata subdivision, the Act extends some of the provisions applicable to body corporates and centre managers. Some of the bylaws of a body corporate may also apply to the lease. Tenants are advised always to ask for a copy of the body corporate bylaws to ascertain if there are any liabilities that may be

passed on to the tenant, particularly major repair, and maintenance and body corporate fees.

QUEENSLAND

- If the store is over 1000m2 in size and is leased to a public company, it does not fall under the Act.
- Stores over 10,000 m2 in size leased to any person or company also do not fall under the Act.
- The Act also does not apply to franchised service stations governed by the Petroleum Retail Marketing Franchise Act.
- Leases for fewer than 6 months are exempted from most of the provisions of the Act.
- A lease can be terminated by the tenant within 6 months of the lease been entered into, if the landlord fails to provide a disclosure statement, or such statement is incomplete, or materially false or misleading.
- Within 30 days after signing the lease the landlord must supply the tenant with a certified copy of the lease. If the landlord fails to do this he can be fined.
- Unlike the other states, where 5 years is the minimum lease period that must be offered to the tenant, Queensland has no minimum period for the lease.
- In the event of a specialist valuer being used to determine the market rent for the premises, each party must pay for half the valuer's fee.
- Land Tax is not recoverable from tenants if they fall under the Act.
- A landlord can charge a tenant for the supply of electricity to the premises based on charges under the Electricity Act in that state. Tenants should always request that the rate for electricity should be at the same rate as paid by the landlord or the best rate.
- Where the tenant supplies the landlord with sales figures for percentage rent purposes, the landlord may not disclose any figures other than those as provided in the Act.
- Unlike Victoria that allows for only one form of rental increase, Queensland permits rental increases to be CPI plus a percentage. A cap on the CPI is permitted under the Act. For example CPI shall be not more than 4% or less than 2%.

- If the lease has a market review of rent clause and if the parties cannot arrive at a figure, the review must be undertaken by a specialist valuer in a manner as set out in the Act.
- If a retailer is buying a business from an existing retailer, and the lease has an option for a further term, and the lease provides for a market rent review on the exercise of such option, the tenant in order to facilitate the sale, may request an early determination of a review in writing. Any notices in this regard, must be not more than 6 months or less than 3 months from the date on which the option is to be exercised.
- While sinking funds are permitted for major repairs and maintenance, any annual sinking fund payment must not exceed 5% of the total estimated outgoings, and the balance in the sinking fund may not at any time exceed $100,000.
- Payment of key money to secure a tenancy is prohibited.
- Rent in advance is limited to one month's rent.
- If a tenant suffers damage as a result of actions by the landlord that disrupt trade or limit access to the premises, the Act sets out how compensation is to be paid, even if the tenants is in a: holding over" period after the expiry of the lease term.
- A landlord may not impose additional restrictions on an assignment of the lease.
- An existing tenant and the guarantor are automatically released from the lease, if on assignment a disclosure statement, and provided to the assignee and provided that any such statements are not misleading or defective.
- If the lease contains an option, the landlord must notify the tenant as to the date after which the option is no longer exercisable, at least 6 months and not more than 12 months before that date.
- If the landlord does not give the notice required, the option remains exercisable until 6 months after the landlord provides the required notice. The lease will then continue under the "holding over" provisions of the lease.
- A clause in a lease is void if it prevents the tenant from joining a tenant's association.
- A provision in a lease that attempts to force a tenant to trade outside the core trading hours is void. In addition, tenants who do not open

their stores are not liable to pay the extra outgoings caused by the tenants that do remain open.

- Disputes about the lease are settled firstly through mediation, and if the dispute is not settled after 4 months, it is referred to the Tribunal where each party pays its own legal costs.
- Unlike in Victoria, the lease can provide that a tenant may have to indemnify a landlord for any damage suffered by the landlord as a result of the tenant's actions.
- Unless a retailer has more than 6 stores in Australia, he may be requested to provide a financial advice and legal advice report to the landlord. A consultant will be of assistance in completing these reports.

The Retail Tenancy Acts in the above 3 states are constantly under review by the State Governments. Any prospective retailer should consult an attorney to ascertain whether the tips suggested in this book are valid or whether case law and the Act may have changed.

PART 2
LEASE NEGOTIATION

PART 3

EXITING FROM
YOUR BUSINESS

CHAPTER 43

THE DECISION TO RETIRE AND EXIT FROM YOUR BUSINESS

Are you reaching the stage of life when you wish you could escape the everyday confines of your business, play golf or be out on the bay? Or are you a franchisee who has had enough of franchising and would like to move on?

Do not walk away from something you've spent so much of your time and energy establishing. Approach this change in your business life like all others - in a logical and planned manner. In this way you can achieve the best outcome.

The following chapters will take you through the many aspects that you and your family need to carefully consider and review before it is time for you to call in your lawyer or financial planner.

WHAT ARE THE MAIN OPTIONS FACING THE OWNER WHEN HE DECIDES TO LEAVE THE BUSINESS?

When an owner of a business leaves, he or she has 3 options and each of these brings its own problems.

1. Sell the Business.
2. A management buyout by staff.
3. Keeping it in the family.

SALE OF BUSINESS

- If you sell the business, you will realise its value without the demand of transition.
- However, the owner must be ready to disengage from the business almost immediately.
- Sometimes, new owners will ask the current owner to stay on in an advisory capacity, and the owner will have to learn to deal with the style of the new management.
- A sale would require the business to be made ready for sale and due diligence by a new owner. We will deal with this in more detail later.

MANAGEMENT BUY-OUT

- This will give your existing staff even more incentive to further the business' profitability.
- It may be a good strategy for the existing owner to remain on as a board member or having a less active role, without walking away from the business completely.
- There would be less argument as to price, as all parties would be aware of the company's progress, strengths and weaknesses. They would also have relatively similar views on its value.
- Banks may be happy to support this approach, as it involves less risk than dealing with new or unfamiliar management.

KEEPING IT IN THE FAMILY

- This can be a difficult proposition particularly for large families taking into consideration the aspirations of the potential heirs.
- Communication is the essential ingredient, and the need to cater for those family members who may miss out must be handled with the utmost delicacy.
- The equal share basis may not always be the best way to go. A business must have people who can assume leadership, make quick decisions, and ensure that the business is focused on its objectives. Management by committee does not always allow for this.
- The different talents and capabilities of all heirs should be fully and unemotionally resolved. The need to broaden the experience of

successors, who may have technical but not financial backgrounds, should also be fully explored.

- The possibility of a successor working in another company in the industry to broaden his skills could be considered.
- The use of a form of mentoring offered by many companies to assist the overall skills of the individuals, who will be running the company in the future, is worth considering,

WHY DO MANY RETAILERS HAVE TROUBLE FACING THE ISSUE OF SUCCESSION PLANNING?

With the ageing of the Australian population, many owners of retail businesses may be faced with having to plan for retirement and ensuring an orderly succession to the next generation.

History tells us that family owned businesses fail more often then they succeed. The average life cycle of a family business is 27 years, which means that many family orientated businesses never make it past the first generation.

Many Australian small businesses tend to put succession planning on the back burner. This is probably the reason why 70% of small family businesses never make it to the second generation. Only 13% are run by grandchildren and less than 3% are run by great grandchildren.

These statistics show that that much of the family wealth created in the first generation is frequently lost by the third generation. There are many reasons suggested for this phenomenon:

- There is often a perceived conflict in values and beliefs between generations about leadership styles.
- Succeeding generations that now own the business, may experience family problems such as divorce or the death of a spouse. A family problem soon becomes a business problem, particularly if these new owners cannot fulfill their obligations in their management roles.

The only way for a sustainable cross generation family business to succeed is to have continuity. This must be consciously led and managed and can best be achieved by:

257

PART 3
EXITING FROM YOUR BUSINESS

- Maximizing effective communication through shared values and building a sense of community.
- Growing the family's human and intellectual capital.
- Mentoring the existing family members to build confidence in their new roles and eliminate any management weaknesses.

Retirement is hard to envisage when there is still so much to do, and succession planning has a ring of finality to it.

A study conducted by KPMG some years ago, showed that for most family businesses, succession planning is a key issue. It raises sensitive issues about the future of the business, the potential crystallisation of tax liabilities, the distribution of wealth accumulated in the business and the relationships between family members.

Only 15% of the surveyed businesses reported having a formal business plan, although 31% said that they were currently working on one. In addition, over 40% of respondents intended to pass on the business to the next generation or other family members. Nearly 20% admitted to having changed their succession plans during the previous 12 months.

It is possible, that the recent financial crisis and Covid-19, may well have delayed succession moves in some businesses by increasing uncertainty and reducing financial flexibility.

Statistics show that despite the world economic crisis, over the next 5 years more than 50% of Australian family business CEO's will retire. Only about 65% have identified their successor and just 25% have a documented succession plan in place.

Even though you may be thinking about a succession plan and feel that the future of your business is safe, you will discover that adequate succession planning is far more complex than you imagine.

There are 4 major areas of risk that may upset the most well intended planning:

- Death or illness can come to managers when they least expect it.
- You may not be able to leave the business when you want to for financial or other reasons.

- You may not be able to realise the maximum value of the business when you decide to leave.
- You may not be able to keep the business running without being actively present.

How you manage these risks depends on your personal objectives. There is no one size fits all succession plans.

WHAT DOES HAVING A SUCCESSION PLAN SIGNAL TO THE OUTSIDE WORLD?

By carefully planning the next step for your business, you will be sending a signal to the trade, to your competitors, and to the bankers who supply finance to your business, that your business is expected to be successful and thrive into the next generation.

This signal indicates that the next generation has been trained, and can take over the business in the event of the retirement or demise of the current owner. Bankers in particular, feel comfortable when such a plan is in place, particularly in the current retail climate.

A plan will help to clarify the hopes and aspirations of the successors. It will highlight estate planning and retirement issues at an early stage when action can still be taken.

CREATING AN ON-GOING LEGACY

Good succession planning takes care of you, your family and the community that may rely on your business. It is about laying the foundations for the longevity of the business after you have gone, and it secures an exit deal that is good for you and the people you care about. Good succession planning caters for all that occurs in the business, that is both the expected and the unexpected.

A plan is best made early, reviewed regularly, and should be based on sound independent and expert advice.

CHAPTER 44

ARE YOU READY FOR SUCCESSION?

Do not jump into succession planning. Take your time. Answer the following checklist before deciding if this is the path you would like to take and whether you are ready for it.

- Do you view your business as a family business?
- Do you want your business to remain a family business? If so why, and how will you go about maintaining its status?
- Do you have potential successors in mind who are willing and able to manage the business? Are these plans clearly defined?
- Does the business have plans for the career development of successor members? If so what are they?
- If you want fair play, does the business have a formal appraisal and remuneration system for family and non-family members?
- Do you have written personal, family, business and succession plans in place?
- Do your plans cover unforseen events?
- Do your plans include death, disability and business continuity insurance policies? If so, what are these details?
- Is the business adequately resourced and staffed to cope with growth in the long term, as well as the short term?
- Do you have a board of directors or advisory board to guide the younger business owner and help him/her where required?
- Do you have agreed processes for handling conflicts between family

and business issues, and between family members? If so, what are they?

If most of your answers are positive and you have a clear and logical plan for future succession, you are ready to take the next step and look at implementation.

ESTABLISH A SUITABLE STRUCTURE FOR YOUR BUSINESS

Whether your eventual goal is selling the business or finding a new manager, either from your family, or from external sources (but retaining ownership and some level of income), you will need to structure the company so that it can function without you.

This structure should entail the following:

- Formal governance systems.
- Well documented systems and processes.
- Formal contracts to lock in key staff, customers, and suppliers.
- Registering all your intellectual property and trade names.
- Having a secure long-term lease in place.

Depending on the size of your business, there are some other considerations before embarking on your plans. These include the following:

- Do you have a clear retirement plan? Has this plan been implemented?
- Is your retirement income adequately funded?
- Does your family and business have a clear mission statement or policy charter? If so, what is it?
- Have you discussed your succession plans with your spouse or partner?
- Does your spouse or partner share your vision of the future?
- What are the largest risks to your business?
- How are you managing the aspirations of your staff?
- Do you have in place a business plan and cash forecast for the company to cover the short- and long-term projections of the business?
- Do you know how to structure your business to get the best tax outcome from the sale?

- What type of management information do you generate every month?

If your answer is NO to many of these questions, you may have some thinking to do followed by extensive planning. If your plan is to sell the business, you will need to put in the time to prepare the business to withstand a significant due diligence test from a buyer. Purchasers are all too aware that in a small business most of the goodwill sits with the owner.

SETTING THE DATE FOR YOUR RETIREMENT WITH YOUR FAMILY

- The first step in succession planning is setting a retirement date target.
- The next step involves a meeting of the family to discuss your retirement and its implications.
- Simply walking away is not a solution. This is a family decision and joint project, in which everyone starts to mentally prepare for the retirement of the owner.
- Every family business is different, and you must now separate business issues from personal issues. For example, sale to a brother could upset the owner's son or the brother's children.
- Once the retirement date has been set, some estate planning considerations can be put into place in consultation with legal and financial advisers.
- Having enough money to retire, may drive succession planning. This may be the case, if the principal feels that more money can be raised by either selling the business or listing it on the stock exchange (if large enough), rather than by bequeathing to children with a guaranteed income stream from the business.
- A good succession plan could take several years to prepare and implement, and once agreed upon, all the family must be committed to it.

CHAPTER 45

MENTORING FAMILY MEMBERS

We all know of successful businesses where children have followed in a father's footsteps and within a short period of time the business has failed or has been sold short of its value.

This is not what you want for your business.

One of the questions facing a company that decides on a likely successor for the current CEO from the family unit, is will the new person have the capabilities and management skills to run the business as well as the existing CEO.

The new person may have strong selling or buying skills, but may lack financial skills. The sudden mantle of leadership may be overwhelming. No one can know or do it all. Mentors and mentoring has been around since the beginning of time, and can help you to educate the successor in your business in any areas of deficiency.

WHAT IS MENTORING, AND HOW CAN YOU FIND THE CORRECT MENTOR?

- A mentor is simply a role model to consult for advice, guidance, and support.
- There are many mentors offering their services in Australia. But, before engaging one, you need to assess and consider the strengths and weaknesses of the potential new CEO, both generally and from a business perspective. Only then can you conclude the way in

which a mentor may help the new CEO to grow both personally and professionally.

- It may also be worth considering what sort of person you are and the type of mentor who compliments you.
- Possibly, the hardest part of the mentoring process will be finding a genuine and talented mentor. A number of government authorities provide successful business people to mentor small business owners.
- Informal mentoring relationships can also be extremely beneficial. A good idea, is to network and join industry associations and make contacts. You may identify businesses you admire and then consider contacting them.
- When you discover someone with whom you would like to develop a mentoring relationship, take things slowly. First ask that person to lunch or send them an email that asks a specific question. Gauge the attractiveness of the person as a mentor based on their response and the value of their advice. Just as you do not propose marriage to somebody on the first date, you should not ask somebody if they will be your mentor straight away.
- Remember, working with a mentor is the best way to get an unofficial business education. Therefore, it is essential that you can feel that you can be open and honest with this person. You need to feel free to ask them your questions. They need to understand your dreams for the business.
- Ultimately, the level of communication you have with your mentor will determine the success of the relationship.
- The mentoring relationship usually lasts from about 6 months to a year. If you are grooming a successor to a family business this could take longer. There is nothing to stop you cultivating another relationship with another mentor as well who meets your changing needs and the needs of your business.
- While you soak up your mentor's knowledge, you cannot simply meet with him or her, sit in a chair and hope that their knowledge will transfer to you like a sponge. Make the most of your limited time with your mentor by dealing with two or three issues at the most that you want help with. Work on the knowledge you have gained and assess your progress together. The progress of the succession plan depends on this.

CHAPTER 46

SUCCESSION AND RETIREMENT TECHNIQUES THAT MAKE FULL USE OF YOUR RETAIL LEASE

Before leaving a business, always consider the range of techniques available that could boost the financial viability of your business. The following are some suggestions that you might think about and then discuss with your accountant or lawyer:

USING YOUR RETAIL LEASE TO MAXIMUM ADVANTAGE

As the lease is often the single item that under-pins the value of your business, you need to examine it and ask yourself the following questions:

- Do I have a solid retail lease, and does it maximize the value of my business?
- What will the buyer of a business be looking for when conducting the proper due diligence on an existing lease?
- If the retail store is located on real estate owned by me, how can I improve the value of that real estate by using my lease?
- Can I use the conditions of the lease to create a better tax effective dissolution of a partnership?

PUTTING THE LEASE IN ORDER WITH A VIEW TO A SALE OF YOUR BUSINESS

As indicated earlier in the book, just as you need to have a good lease entering a business, so you need to ensure that you have a good lease exiting a business. The buyer's solicitor will be looking at several key items in the lease in order to determine this.

The following are key issues which makes the lease a good lease for a new buyer:

- It should have at least 5 years to run until the end of the current lease term.
- If possible, it should have an option for one or two additional lease terms. Such options should be totally unrestricted in their ability to be exercised.
- If your lease has only a short time to go, no buyer trying to assess the potential of the business will be prepared to pay for goodwill knowing that within a short period he may no longer have a lease.
- If you have an old lease which commenced before the introduction of changes to state acts, ensure that the outgoings clause does not have a provision requiring you to pay for the shortfall in outgoings that have not been paid by the major tenants.
- Ensure that any market review clauses have no "ratchet clauses" which only allows rental to rise following a review. In tough times market rentals usually fall. The new rental determined by a market review must be allowed to fall to this new level.
- Ensure that clauses dealing with repainting and restoration are not at fixed intervals, but "as and when necessary."
- Ensure that no immediate fit out of the business is required on assignment, as this will be considered by a potential buyer in assessing the purchase price for the retail business.
- Ensure that if the store is situated in a regional shopping centre, the total gross rent, comprising base rent, variable outgoings, statutory charges and marketing contribution, does not exceed the benchmark for that category. This information can be obtained from the URBIS annual reports on occupancy costs.

ASK YOURSELF THE FOLLOWING QUESTIONS:

Have the premises been surveyed, and is there a survey certificate attached to the lease. Since rent and outgoings are measured on a rate per square metre, it is vital that the area as shown in the lease is correct.

Is there a cap on the "making good provision" in the lease, or will the buyer be faced with a costly removal expense for items like partitions and counters ,as well as the cost of returning the premises to its original state? A photo of the premises at the date of initial handover would be useful.

In Victoria, ensure that if there is to be a market review on the exercise of the option in the lease, and that there is a provision for the market review to be completed first before you have to exercise your option.

INITIATING AN EARLY LEASE NEGOTIATION

If you are contemplating a sale of the business and you have only 2 years to go on the lease with no further option, it is imperative that you initiate negotiations with your landlord for a new lease as soon as possible. The longer you leave it, the more difficult it will be to achieve your desired outcome.

The recent amendments to the retail tenancy legislation in some states set out the legal position regarding early lease negotiation and should be used as a guide for the sale of the business. This applies particularly when there is one year to run plus a 5-year option in your lease. If the lease requires a market review on the exercise of the option, such review should be executed as early as possible, and the market review used as the rental for the start of the option period.

A retailer planning retirement, has nothing to fear when opening negotiations with a landlord to initiate a new lease. This should be an opportunity to reset the level of occupancy cost for a number of years to come.

WHAT ABOUT BUSINESS OWNERS WHO HAVE GIVEN PERSONAL GUARANTEES ON A LEASE?

The giving of a personal guarantee on the lease by the directors or shareholders of a tenant in a retail business has become standard practice. But what happens if the guarantor wishes to retire?

In practice, most landlords will accept the removal of a guarantor on a lease where the owner is retiring, and the business is to be continued by the owner's children.

It is essential that the process is handled formally by the tenant's solicitor acting on behalf of the family. The full details of your exit must be outlined as well as the way the family business will continue to be managed. It must be made clear that the children will replace the father as the guarantor on the lease. It is essential, that the solicitor makes clear that this change will not affect the landlord's security on the lease.

USING THE LEASE TO HAVE A TAX EFFECTIVE AND FINANCIALLY EQUITABLE DISSSOLUTION OF A PARTNERSHIP

In some instances, the partners in a business, whether in a strip centre or stand-alone property, have bought the real estate in which the business is operating. In some cases, the partners have been paying a predetermined rental to the company owning the real estate.

Where one partner intends to take over the business and the other wants to acquire the real estate as his or her "superannuation nest egg", the structuring of the lease for the business to continue can be tax effective. It can also allow each partner to meet their own individual goals and objectives.

My comments previously dealing with the creating of a lease for the premises where you own the property from which you run your business to improve the value of your family assets, should be reviewed when planning your retirement.

CHAPTER 47

CAPITAL GAINS TAX CONCESSIONS AVAILABLE TO SMALL BUSINESSES ON THE SALE OF A BUSINESS

As with all business matters, the more you understand, the better your situation while operating your business, and later when leaving it. Capital Gains Tax concerns are a complex area, but worth your attention even before consulting your tax adviser.

It is essential that you obtain tax advice in respect of any Capital Gains Tax that may arise on the sale of your business. The following is a guide for discussion with your tax adviser:

Being aware of the small business CGT concessions of Division 152 of the Income Tax Assessment Act, is important for retailers contemplating a sale of the business. This allows you to sell your businesses free from CGT, or at least at a greatly reduced CGT cost.

WHAT IS THE SMALL BUSINESS RETIREMENT EXEMPTION?

The small business retirement exemption, allows qualifying taxpayers to make a capital gain of up to $500,000 without paying any GST, if the relevant requirements are met. Your tax adviser will advise you of the details of the formula and how to apply it to your business.

SOME OTHER CGT CONCESSIONS AVAILABLE ON SALE OF ASSETS

If your business has owned an asset for 15 years and you are aged 55 years or over and you are retiring, or if you are permanently incapacitated, you will not have an assessable capital gain when you sell the asset

A capital gain from the sale of a business asset will be exempt up to a lifetime limit of $500,000. If you are under 55 years of age, the exempt amount must be paid into a complying superannuation fund or a retirement savings account to obtain the exemption.

If you sell a small business asset you can defer the capital gain for a year later.

CHAPTER 48

LEASE REVIEW BY THE BUYER ON THE PURCHASE OF THE BUSINESS?

In arriving at the final selling price of your business, it would be prudent for a potential buyer to carry out a thorough due diligence on the lease or leases underpinning the purchase of the business.

Several provisions contained in the lease may need to be taken into account in the final purchase price. These include:

- Whether the lease provides for a refit of the premises at the end of the current lease term. If it does, it may entail the purchaser having to spend $100000 to $150000 of his own funds within a short time of taking over the business. This may mean that an appropriate sum of money may have to be deducted from the purchase price.
- Given the flat retail conditions in some centres, the business could have been enjoying a marketing or rental abatement from the landlord of say about $2500 per month being credited to the monthly statement. This will mean that the rental paid as per the profit and loss presented is understated.
- Often these abatements will cease on assignment. Such credits should be reinstated and deducted from the profit of the business before applying the "return on investment" percentage.
- Many leases provide for the painting of the store every 3 years. This may well cost up to $5000 for each job. If the date for painting has not yet been reached before the takeover, an equivalent sum should be considered in the purchase price.

- If the purchase of a business is in a rising rental market where the lease calls for a market review to take place after the date the new buyer has taken over, the purchaser should ask an independent valuer what the market rent is likely to be.
- A possible substantial increase in the market rental will affect the future profitability of the business and should be considered when determining the profitability on which the ROI will be calculated.
- Some leases stipulate that on assignment of the lease, an automatic market review may be triggered. You need to ensure that if this is the case, a valuer can confirm what the rent is likely to be on a market review. This should also be considered in the profitability of the business.
- It is important to ascertain the "vintage" of the lease. If you have an old lease and are currently in the second option period, you could be stuck with all the old provisions of the various state acts, and this could be disadvantageous to the new buyer. It may well be a negotiating point for the buyer to rather negotiate a new lease than live with a "bad" old lease.
- If the business is in a centre which is likely to be refurbished or upgraded shortly, there may be certain outgoings such as building maintenance, air conditioning being upgraded, or a new centre owner substantially increasing management costs. All these items will cause an increase in future outgoings costs and need to be considered in assessing the real future occupancy costs of the business.
- All leases allow for a "make good" provision at the end of the lease. If your business has been restructured to suit the needs of your current store, there could be a substantial cost involved in returning the store to its original condition. At the point of hand over, ask for any existing photos in existence at the date of hand over. This will allow the purchaser to ascertain the potential liability at the end of the lease.

CHAPTER 49

PLANNING FOR SUCCESSION IF YOU HAVE A BUSINESS PARTNER

The retirement or death of your business partner can be very distressing on a personal level. It can also cause havoc in your business if the necessary business plans and agreements for a smooth and trouble-free hand over are not in place.

One of the best approaches is for the partners to put into place a buy/sell agreement which is sometimes known as a "cross purchase contract" that establishes the legal structure by which ownership is transferred.

Though you may have liked your partner as a friend and trusted him completely, can you be so sure about his wife or children? Too many disputes on partnership succession finish up in the courts and involve all parties with substantial legal fees.

It is advisable that a complete business succession partnership plan be drawn up by a competent accountant, supported by solid legal advice where necessary. This may cost a few thousand dollars, but it could be the best investment of your life. It will give all parties peace of mind and avoid the conflict and cost that could occur on the departure of a partner.

WHAT SHOULD BE CONTAINED IN A BUY/SELL AGREEMENT

- It should cover all situations of possible departure including:

273

retirement, death, illness, bankruptcy of a partner, insanity, and criminal conviction.

- It must be drawn up in line with the rules that govern the partnership, such as the partnership agreement or articles of association, if it is a company.
- It must be flexible enough to cover the entry of new partners and exit of existing partners.
- It must be unambiguous and easily understood by all parties.
- It must clearly set out the precise chain of events that are to take place to facilitate the departure of a partner and the transfer or sale of the business to the remaining partners or to third parties.
- It must include a timetable to bring effect to the transfer.
- It should recognize specific periods of mourning as per the religious denominations of the partners.
- It must address the concerns of capital gains tax, stamp duty and other tax considerations. This part of the agreement should be constantly amended as tax legislation changes.
- It must recognize the problem of funding to pay out a partner or his estate, and this may include taking out life policies and/or setting up of annuities to meet the needs of the remaining or surviving partners.

HOW BEST TO APPROACH AND IMPLEMENT THE STRUCTURE OF THE BUY SELL AGREEMENT

Although solicitors and accountants may suggest different approaches, the form of the agreement you follow depends on your relationship with your partner. It may include creating mutual wills or conditional contracts of purchase. From my experience, the agreement that seems to work best is the "options basis".

This works in the following way:

- Each partner grants the other an option to purchase each other's interest in the business on the occurrence of an event as contained in the agreement. These options are both a *put* and a *call* option.
- The options are worded so that the amount of the interest has been

predetermined at a fixed price, or market price established by a recognized broker, acceptable to both parties.

- The option must also bind the executor of each partner's estate. (At present a transfer at a market price may not be subject to stamp duty but that should be checked with your legal adviser in each state).
- The option should be personal to each partner, and until such time as the option is formally exercised, each partner should retain his full interest in the partnership.
- Funding of the buy-out as indicated above, may be by way of a term life policy on each partner's life or a form of annuity.

PLANNING TO BRING A JUNIOR PARTNER INTO YOUR BUSINESS

Most exit strategies are put in place several years prior to the voluntary departure of an owner. Therefore, if you feel that you would like to have that "trial run" of what it's like to play golf on one or two days a week, do not rush out and sell, but consider the option of possibly taking on a junior partner.

However, consider the following:

- Nobody likes to have a minority interest in a business. To entice a good junior partner, you may have to offer an interest of about 20% – 25% with the option to buy out the balance within 5 years. All details of succession need to be fully documented, as indicated previously, with a proper buy and sell agreement.
- A junior partner may inject into the business a new degree of enthusiasm, which may enhance the business and its eventual value on a sell out.
- Remember, a junior partner, like the owner, is reviewing several considerations about buying the junior partnership. Some of these will include: -

1. Not being locked into a minority position with small equity and little management input without the opportunity to increase equity in the future.
2. Whether he will be able to get along with the senior partner and they will work well together.

3. The junior partner will view it as an opportunity not otherwise available whilst the owner gets a "ready buyer" for the business. Thus, it can prove to be a "win-win" situation for both parties.

CHAPTER 50

SELLING THE BUSINESS OUTRIGHT

As you approach retirement you may arrive at the decision that you wish to sell the business.

We will look at the actual process of selling your business under the following topic headings: -

- Planning an exit strategy from the business to achieve a successful outcome, including key issues that will be addressed by the purchaser and strategies to be avoided that will hold up the final sale.
- Appointing and managing a broker during the selling process.
- Determining the worth of the business and the return on investment a potential buyer will be willing to pay.
- Working with a broker to determine the most effective break up of the final selling price, between stock, fixtures, fittings and goodwill.
- Working with a broker to create a good marketing document that displays the business in the best possible light to a potential buyer.
- Minimizing capital gains tax from the sale of the business.
- Preparing the business for sale, including putting your stock in order and bringing up to date fixtures and fittings schedules.

PLANNING THE EXIT STRATEGY

To conclude a successful sale of your business, always put yourself in the place of the buyer and try to look at things from his perspective. Think like a buyer and not a seller.

What issues are important to the buyer?

A potential buyer will always consider any risks facing your business at present. Therefore, if for any reason, your business is at risk you need to ask yourself the following:

- Do your customers have a relationship with you and not your company?
- Is your supply chain held together with handshakes and "gentlemen's agreements" and not contracts?
- Are you the only person who knows how every bit of the business works?
- Do your key staff only stay out of loyalty to you?
- Is your Intellectual property in your head?
- Are you using your personal assets as security for your business?
- Do you have contingency plans or a disaster recovery plan?

Unless your business can run without you, a new buyer may only pay for what he believes the business is worth. You may need to negotiate to stay on for a defined period. To get the best price you may have to wait on the market. You definitely do not want to sell at the bottom of the market.

The following are the key issues that most purchasers of a business will want to address:

- Is the price reasonable?
- What are the key "deal breakers" from the buyer's point of view, which will make or break the deal?
- Is the acquisition properly structured?
- What are the sustainable levels of profit and cash flow for your shop?
- If the buyer owns another shop what additional benefits will the acquisition mean for both businesses?
- What are the taxation implications of the acquisition?
- What is the true value of the assets?
- Does the business have proper systems and controls, and have the figures been correctly audited?

- What are the working capital requirements of the business? If the buyer needs to up-size and put in more stock, will he get assistance from my suppliers?
- How much more capital is needed for fixed assets like a new refit of the premises that may be required under the lease?
- Is there an implementation strategy to ensure that the business operates as planned from day one of the acquisition?

FROM YOUR POINT OF VIEW AS THE SELLER

Making a snap decision that it is time to sell is not prudent.

If you cannot meet the needs of a buyer as set out above, you will not be able to sell your business to its full value and potential.

Remember, that it is critical for the business to show potential to a future buyer, so that he will be willing to pay you goodwill.

THE KEY INGREDIENTS FOR A PLANNED EXIT STRATEGY

- Planning for your exit should be initiated at least 3 to 5 years prior to you exiting the business.
- Invest in proper financial controls and up to date point of sale cash registers capable of analysing sales and gross profits on each item sold by department or product group.
- Have your books audited, and have a full set of audited results prepared by a qualified firm of auditors.
- Prepare a budget and a 5-year business plan to be updated annually for the next 5 years.
- Set up an organized open to buy planning system. In this way you can control your purchases to ensure that markdowns are kept to a minimum and gross profits do not fluctuate widely.
- Take a full inventory of your fixtures and fittings with their cost price and a noted value. Your tax returns will be a useful place to ascertain dates of purchase of these fixed assets and their original cost price.
- Enter the inventory into a fixed asset register to be kept until the sale of the business, or as you acquire new assets.

- As indicated earlier, ensure that your lease is in order and has several years to run, or contains unconditional options which can be exercised by the new purchaser.
- To enhance the value of the business, it may be worthwhile becoming a member of a marketing group.
- If there are plans to re-route a road near your business or a possible relocation of your store in a shopping centre, make certain that you are aware of all the facts. Do not wait for the purchaser to tell you about it during negotiations. Your local council offices may be extremely helpful in this regard.
- Finally, contact a broker recommended to you by another retailer satisfied with the sale of their business and the price obtained.

APPOINTING A BROKER AND MANAGING THE BROKER DURING THE SELLING PROCESS

When you are confident that the business is ready for sale, set the "bush telegraph" into operation by telling your colleagues that your business may be for sale, if you receive the right offer.

The moment you decide to sell your shop you are faced with 2 options: -

1. Do I try to conclude the sale myself and save the commission on the sale.

OR

2. Do I contact a broker and let him do the job for me and pay the commission.

From my experience, I find that brokers are professionals at their job of selling a business. The commission that you pay them will more than covered in the price you receive. A broker will be able to sort out the genuine buyers from the rest.

There are several steps that ought to be taken into consideration when dealing with a broker, so that he carries out the sale according to your wishes.

These include the following:

- Determining the type of broker you want to deal with. Meet with a number of brokers and select the one you feel most comfortable with before making the appointment.
- Prior to the appointment, it is wise to prepare a document of sale which can be used by the broker as part of the selling process.

This document should include the following:

- The selling price that you believe the shop is worth.
- Your means of allocating the price between stock, fixtures, fittings and goodwill.
- An available layout of the store together with a location plan.
- A copy of the lease, and if you are in the process of negotiations, copies of the latest correspondence with the landlord.
- A copy of the audited accounts of the shop for the past 3 years.
- A trend analysis showing growth patterns of sales and profits over the last 3 years, to demonstrate to a potential buyer a strong profitable business.
- Some colour photos of the premises from both outside and inside.

Use your accountant or a business adviser to critically analyse and assess your information and the financial data used in support of your valuation.

Having decided on the broker you prefer, take the documents with your views about the sale, to the broker for initial discussion.

Discuss the document in detail with the broker and take into consideration his analysis of the market and his assessment of your business potential. You will need to have a flexible approach and be prepared to amend your expectations on the selling price. No doubt you will be able to assess whether the broker is an expert in the area.

It is important not to set your expectations too high. Often the initial discussion can be very distressing. No store owner is happy to hear that their life's work is not worth as much as they thought it was.

- Once you have the broker's commitment to the sale, and you have both agreed on an approximate selling price, confirm his appointment in writing. Clarify whether he is hired exclusively or for a period of months.

- Ensure that any potential buyers that the broker introduces to you are prepared to make an offer in your price range.
- Once the deal is concluded, ensure that the broker is paid his commission in full.

CHAPTER 51

VALUATION OF THE BUSINESS

It is accepted in the industry that a retail business is usually valued on a return-on-investment basis.

This method is determined by the following procedures: -

- Taking the adjusted net profit of the business as per the audited accounts.
- Deducting an appropriate salary for the owner/managers.
- The resulting figure is called the return on investment or R.O.I.
- The R.O.I is now multiplied by 100 and divided by the required return which gives us the total purchase price of the business.

Example:

If after your accountant has made the appropriate adjustments to net profit before tax by deducting extraneous income and adding back deductions (that would not apply to the new business), you have a net profit before tax of $200000.

The business is one with potential in a good location, with a good lease in place and a low risk attached to it and a return of 18% is considered appropriate.

The manager or owner of the business earns a salary of $50000 per annum.

Then the ROI will be   200000 – 50000.

                              = 150000

The value of the business Will be

$$\frac{150000 \times 100}{18}$$

$$= \$833333$$

Thus, on an investment of \$833333, the new buyer will receive a return of 18% on his investment.

The professionalism of the broker

The crucial element is to know what percentage returns to apply. And this is where the professionalism of the broker comes in to play.

In times of high interest rates up to 25% ROI can be anticipated. In a low interest market as at present, 15% may be sufficient, considering a risk factor over the current interest rates.

The question people often ask a broker or adviser is, how do I assess the future potential of the business?

In assessing potential there are a few elements to be considered, such as:

- The sales growth of the business over the past 3 to 5 years.
- The quality of the competition in the area or shopping centre.
- The traffic flow movements to the shopping centre over the past 3 years.
- The population increases and developments in the area.

Once you have established the purchase price of the business, you now must break up this price into its three components namely.

- Stock
- Value of Fixtures and Fittings
- Goodwill

A. VALUATION OF STOCK

The valuation of stock usually refers to the valuation on the day of sale.

However, the valuation can also be fairly accurately calculated from the retailers own audited profit and loss account.

The valuation is calculated by taking the average of the opening and closing stocks as shown in the previous accounts.

Example:

Stock at the Start of the year	= $100500
Closing Stock For Year	= $110700
	$211200
$211200 divided by 2	= $105600 Average
Rounded off the value of stock is:	$106000

B. VALUATION OF FIXTURES AND FITTINGS

There are two basic methods of arriving at the value of the fixtures and fittings:

Estimating the written down value of the assets as per the fixed asset register or as per the retailers' tax file forming a support schedule to the tax return for the business.

OR

Estimating the market value of the fixtures and fittings.

The advantage from the seller's point of view, of using the written down value, is that this results in no capital gains tax payable on the difference between the written down value and the market value.

The assets may be worth a lot more than their written down value. This method may be preferable as it more accurately reflects what a willing buyer would pay in a sale of an ongoing business.

In addition, the higher the value of the fixtures and fittings, the more the seller will be able to claim as a reduction for taxation (in respect of depreciation on such higher assets.)

No stamp duty is payable on the fixtures and fittings component of the sale, so this is a further incentive to value fixtures and fittings at "best" market value.

C. GOODWILL

The value of the stock, plus the agreed value of the fixtures and fittings subtracted from the total price as assessed, gives the goodwill component of the price.

GST

If the business is sold as a going concern it will not attract GST. However, if the taxation office determines that the sale of the business was not a genuine sale "of a going concern", the sale of the property will be liable for GST.

If the vendor assumes that the sale is a going concern, but the tax office rules that it is not, the vendor will be left bearing the cost of the GST. This may or may not be later recoverable from the buyer. It is advisable to check this point with your tax adviser.

It is worth considering that in order to obtain the GST exemption, the tax office has ruled in advance that a vendor can supply leased premises as part of the sale of the business as a going concern, by either assigning the existing lease or arranging for the lessor to grant a new lease before the completion date. Similar treatment will also apply to franchise agreements.

The tax office has relaxed its views regarding the transfer of employees as a requirement for a going concern. However, if "key employees" have skills or knowledge that are essential to the continued operation of the going concern, that knowledge or skill should be transferred. The new employer is not required to employ the key staff members.

Once again check these points with your tax adviser.

CHAPTER 52

SPENDING AND INVESTING YOUR MONEY

Congratulations! You have now sold your business, and now you have the pleasant task of deciding what you are going to do with the money.

Planning your finances for retirement is essential. If done properly and with care, you can be assured of a retirement free from financial worry.

Building a successful financial plan involves assessing the funds you have now, deciding on your needs for the future and how long your money needs to last.

I suggest that you appoint a financial adviser but this is often not as easy as it seems.

In selecting an adviser, the following criteria should be met: -

- The adviser must be a person who will continue to take care of you long after your investments have been placed.
- He must be a licensed dealer with the Australian Securities Commission.
- Some advisers may only have a licence restricted to dealing in certain specific investments or securities. Ask your adviser if his license has any restrictions.
- Your adviser should be qualified and involved in ongoing training to ensure that he is abreast of the latest legislation and investment strategies.

- Make sure that your adviser has the resources and research facilities to keep abreast of happenings in the investment market and the economy, as well as changes in taxation and financial legislation.
- Be certain that your adviser agrees to send you regular reports and financial statements and that he will keep in contact with you if any changes or opportunities arise that may affect your financial position.

PAYING YOUR ADVISER

Before you ask an adviser to develop a financial plan for you, ascertain how he will be paid and determine the payment options available to you.

Financial advisers are usually paid in the following ways: -

- The whole question of financial advisor fees has been amended by the government, and you need to be fully familiar with the new regulations before you discuss the question of fees with your adviser.
- The adviser is paid by way of a commission when he places your investment with an investment company. The commission is paid to the adviser by the investment company from the entry fee that the investment company deducts when you invest. The commission is not usually charged as an extra cost to you.
- If you were to approach the investment company directly without using your adviser, you would still be charged the same entrance fee with no commission payable. Therefore, it is no cheaper to go directly to the company or via the adviser.
- The adviser may charge you on a fixed sliding scale, depending on how much you invest and how much time he has taken to work with you. Often an adviser charging a fee will refund to you any commission received from the investment company.

YOUR PLAN

Having selected the appropriate investment advisor and concluded your first meeting to discuss your financial position and goals for the future, request a written financial plan for review by yourself and your family.

The plan prepared by the adviser should contain at least the following criteria:

- That all recommendations should be clearly explained and backed up with current research.
- If the investments include the placing of your funds in a managed fund, this should be supported by details of the fund's investment managers as well as a history of their past performance.
- You should be confident that his recommendations offer you the right level of security, and that you will not be putting your money in risky investments, especially in view of the current financial climate.
- The plan includes an estimate of the likely returns that your investment will achieve and when income payments will be received.
- It should outline a detailed explanation of how you can gain access to your funds in an emergency.
- There should be an explanation on how your investments will affect your pension or other government entitlements.
- There must be a clear statement of the cost of implementing the plan, and how and when you are expected to pay the required amounts.
- There should be a disclosure statement showing any commissions that your adviser will receive.
- In essence, the plan should cover all issues that are important to you and your financial future.

WISHING YOU A HAPPY AND ENJOYABLE RETIREMENT!

PART 3
EXITING FROM YOUR BUSINESS

www.ingramcontent.com/pod-product-compliance
Lightning Source LLC
Chambersburg PA
CBHW081459200326
41518CB00015B/2311